DEVELOPING
Science
IN THE PRIMARY CLASSROOM

Wynne Harlen
Sheila Jelly

LONGMAN

Addison Wesley Longman Ltd
Edinburgh Gate, Harlow,
Essex CM20 2JE, England
and Associated Companies throughout the World

ISBN 0582 30851 8

First published 1989
Second edition 1997
Third impression 1998

Printed in Singapore (KKP)

The Publisher's policy is to use paper manufactured
from sustainable forests.

We are grateful to the children and staff at Roger
Ascham Primary School fore their invaluable help in
creating the photography for this book.

Contents

FOREWORD

Although substantial changes and additions to the contents of this book have been made in producing this second edition, its aims and intended readership remain as before. It is essentially a book for those teachers who want to develop their practice in primary science. This may mean making a conscious effort to develop science from the starting points already there, but perhaps unrecognised, or it may mean building confidence to take further the science work already in progress to ensure that children have an opportunity to develop the full range of science skills, attitudes, and ideas.

Development is the theme of the book: development in teachers of a progressive understanding of what science is and what is their role in teaching it. Development for anyone, be they teachers or children, starts from where they are and leads to some progression. Thus there is a progression in this book, taking the reader from a focus on particular activities, to the analysis of these activities and suggestions for dealing with the problems arising, ways of developing activities and organising the work, considering the role of assessment in learning and teaching and planning for children's progression in learning science. In all of this the context is the classroom and the focus the individual teacher, for although the best framework for teacher development may be one where problems are tackled in groups, it is not possible for all to have the benefit of such a context.

The book begins with an attempt to put into plain words the meaning of learning science and technology. These meanings are implicit throughout the rest of the book and indeed provide the basis for the activities and teaching approaches which are proposed. In Chapter 2 some practical investigations for children are introduced, which form a basis for Chapter 3 where checklists are provided for reviewing the children's and the teacher's activities. They are followed by ways of interpreting what is found and suggestions for tackling problems which might be revealed.

Chapter 4 gives a more detailed rationale for the way of working proposed. It argues that certain kinds of experiences and classroom roles are necessary in order for children to have the opportunity of process-based learning. Chapters 5 and 6 are concerned with the practicalities of providing for this kind of learning, dealing first, in Chapter 5, with developing activities from a range of starting points, through a technique of 'skill-scanning questions'. Pros and cons of different ways of incorporating science into the curriculum and of organising children in the classroom are dealt with in the first part of Chapter 6, whilst later parts deal with equipment and resources. Chapters 7 and 8 take up another aspect of the teacher's role which is essential if children are to learn to make sense of the scientific aspect of the world around. The teacher must know where children start from; what their existing skills, attitudes and ideas are. This calls for a particular kind of assessment that is integral to teaching. Ideas about how to carry out this assessment in relation to children's ideas and how to use the information it provides are the concern of Chapter 7, whilst Chapter 8 considers the same matters in relation to children's skills and attitudes.

Chapter 9 takes a broader and slightly more theoretical view of assessment and considers how information gathered for the purpose of helping learning relates to what is needed to summarise children's achievements for purposes of reporting progress and assisting forward planning. Chapter 10 brings together ideas from previous chapters and considers how children's ideas can be built into broader concepts. The role of teachers' own understanding of science is also considered in the context of the full range of kinds of knowledge that teachers need.

Wynne Harlen

1

SCIENCE AND LEARNING SCIENCE

Science as an established part of the primary curriculum

One thing that has changed in the last two decades is that there is no longer any need to justify the place of science in the curriculum of the primary (elementary) school. A good case was made out in the late sixties and early seventies through the work of curriculum projects in several countries, such as *Science 5/13* (1972) in the UK, the *Elementary Science Study* (*ESS*) (1966) and the *Science Curriculum Improvement Study* (1966) in the US, and the *African Primary Science Project* (1969). The value to those children in the classes where science was introduced was widely recognised, but the quality was not matched by the quantity. The need for more children to have an early opportunity to develop their understanding of the world around them and their ways of exploring it prompted HMIs, in their *Primary Education* survey (DES, 1978), to deplore the fact that so few schools had 'effective programmes for the teaching of science'. In 1985, the then DES underlined the importance of including science in children's education from the start, urging that: 'All pupils should be properly introduced to science in the primary school'. Within a few years, this intention was given the backing of legislation in England and Wales in the Education Reform Act which introduced the National Curriculum. The designation of science as a 'core' subject (together with English and mathematics) of the National Curriculum signifies the status it is now given. Similar recognition of the importance of science led to the development of the National Guidelines 5–14 in Scotland, the National Science Education Standards and Benchmarks for Scientific Literacy in the US, and there is now hardly a country that does not specify that science should be introduced before pupils reach the secondary school, even if not all begin from the first year of school.

So the problem now is not one of convincing advisers, headteachers, class teachers and others concerned with children's primary education of the importance of science, nor of identifying overall aims and objectives or what the content should be, in general terms, since these things are set out in the various curriculum documents. But these documents can never indicate *how* to achieve the objectives nor what are appropriate learning experiences for individual schools, classes or children, which are the immediate concerns of teachers. Questions about, for example, how to start new activities, how to respond to the difficult questions children ask, how to advance children's learning and how to know whether it *has* advanced, are questions which remain unanswered by the existence of national or state-wide documents.

Many teachers feel anxious that they should be doing some science, or more science, or different science, with their classes. Appropriate activities for primary children differ from the experiences of secondary school science of many primary teachers, and it is still too early for there to be many practising teachers who experienced active, enquiry-based science in their own primary education. Even the word 'science' may be a source of worry, particularly now that 'technology' (that is, design and technology) has been added to the curriculum and has to be distinguished from but related to science. It is the aim of this book to take away the mystery and to show the meaning of science at the primary level. We will see that science in this context is not about abstract theories and principles, nor is technology in this context about 'high technology', controlled by computers or involving complex machinery.

The best way to this understanding, however, is not to focus on the definition of science and how it relates to and differs from technology, but rather on what we mean by *learning* science and technology.

Learning science

Let's start with learning science. Essentially, at the primary level this involves children finding out about something through their own actions and making some sense of the result through their own thinking. A child might find out how a caterpillar moves by watching it carefully; another might observe a sugar lump breaking up and dissolving in water; another might watch the colours separate out from an ink blot on damp filter paper; all these activities are part of learning science. The actions may seem little more than passively observing, but note that there is always some action before there is anything to observe: the caterpillar has to be placed on a chosen surface, the sugar lump put in the water, the filter paper, water and ink put together in a certain way. Observing is also a more mentally active than passive process, for when we observe, all of us pay attention selectively to some things rather than others and we try to make sense of what we find as we take it in.

Often action is more obviously a part of the finding out, as when the caterpillars are fed in a controlled way to find out if they have food preferences, or the blades of a model windmill are trimmed to try to make them turn faster, or floating plasticine boats are loaded to see if some shapes of boat hold more than others before sinking. In these cases the children are physically active, more obviously doing than just watching, but we shouldn't run away with the idea that this physical activity is the same as scientific activity. Children can be busy without their activity being purposeful in terms of learning science; conversely, they can be learning a great deal of science through observing, reflecting, discussing and reading – when they are mentally active, making sense of things.

It becomes obvious that a mixture of physical and mental activity is what is needed. The essence of scientific activity, however, and usually its starting point, is the encounter between the child and some phenomenon; some face-to-face interaction of children and things around them, from which they can learn directly through their own physical and mental activity.

> It may be the clouds in the sky, or the birds in the undergrowth; it may be a bumblebee on the clover, or a spider in a web, the pollen of a flower, or the ripples in a pond. It may be the softness of a fleece, the 'bang!!' of a drum, or the rainbow in a soap film. From all around comes the invitation; all around sounds the challenge. The question is there, the answer lies hidden, and the child has the key.
>
> (Jos Elstgeest, 1985, p.10)

The child has the key because, as in all learning, no-one can put ready-made ideas and ways of thinking into his or her head. But whether or not children have the opportunity to develop ideas and ways of thinking for themselves depends crucially on their teacher. When children explore the spider's web, the soap bubbles, the ripples on the pond, the ideas they have about these things afterwards will be different from the ideas they had before they had these encounters. They will learn something. But what they learn will depend on many things, particularly on what ideas they had at the start, what they do and how they interpret what they find. In turn, what they do and what they find will depend on the materials that their teacher provides for them to use, the guidance they receive and the encouragement to do such things as think things out, check ideas by going back to the objects, improve their technique for finding out, challenge preconceived ideas. For all these things it is the teacher who holds the key.

Learning technology

From the start it should be clear that much of what is described these days as technology at the primary level has been included for many years under the label of primary science as advocated by projects such as *Science 5/13*, *ESS* and some later curriculum developments. Science and technology are not the same, but they are so interrelated that they are often closely linked, particularly when we are talking about learning in science and learning in technology.

Science, as already discussed, is concerned with understanding the way things are and why they behave as they do. Technology is concerned with finding practical solutions to problems, especially creating something which meets a human need.

Examples of technology in daily life abound, from building bridges and roads, to making artificial heart valves and producing CDs and tapes. In the primary classroom examples are creating working models, devising a home-made timer, making a contraption to test the strength of hair or to compare the strength of nutshells. In all these cases the application of scientific ideas is combined with creative design, and in most cases an element of aesthetic appreciation is involved to make products which are pleasing to look at as well as functional.

So when children are designing and making something, answering questions such as 'How can we do this?' they can be said to be involved in learning technology; if they are experimenting and investigating to answer questions such as 'What happens if?' or, 'What's different and what's the same about these?' they are involved in learning science. It isn't difficult to see that answering the 'how to' questions involves applying ideas learned through answering 'what happens' questions. Similarly, when a product has been achieved – the model windmill or the timer constructed – it can become the object of investigating and further learning in science. Hence the interpenetration of the two kinds of activity.

This discussion of the distinction between learning science and learning technology shows that we can recognise their differences but without separating them in children's learning. Both are necessary to achieve different aims. It is important that teachers distinguish between them in planning and conducting children's activities so that the aims of each can be systematically pursued. So, technology is

not just about making things; and making things from kits, following instructions, is not technology. Technology involves thinking about the most suitable solution to a problem considering the purpose and circumstances, carefully selecting the materials and tools to use, evaluating the effectiveness of what has been made or done, and studying how solutions to practical problems are brought about.

Outcomes of learning primary science

In various ways the national or local curriculum documents indicate the knowledge and understanding of aspects of the world around that science helps children to develop. Broad headings such as the following are often used:

- the characteristics of living things and the processes of life;

- the properties of materials and how they interact;

- the physical processes of forces, movement and energy in its various forms;

- the Earth in space.

Most primary science activities can readily be identified with one or more of these aspects of the physical world, but the more important point is to decide what level of understanding is appropriate for the primary school child. Where to stop?

Understanding for all of us is a continuous process that continues throughout life. There is no one point where we can say that a physical event is completely understood; it is just understood in different ways at different times. Think of what is meant by 'dissolving' or 'reflection', for example, and how this meaning changes for the young child, for the teenager and for the adult scientist. Reflection is just about shiny surfaces at first, then becomes something that happens at all surfaces whether shiny or not and later it is related to energy transfer at the interface between media. At each stage the level of understanding needed is that which helps the person make sense of his or her experience. So it is with primary children. The development of understanding helps them make sense of what they experience and what they find out through investigation of the scientific aspects of the world around.

This development is something that we return to in Chapter 4. At this point it is important to note that the understanding is dependent upon the process of 'making sense' of what is found through investigation. Thus the development of the abilities to investigate and to interpret what is found are equally important outcomes of primary science. Children need to develop skills of

● testing ideas to see if they fit the evidence;

● collecting evidence by observation and investigation;

● interpreting evidence and relating what is found to initial ideas;

● relating ideas from one situation to help understanding and investigation of another situation.

Whilst involved in the processes of finding out and solving problems (and learning how to do these more effectively) children will implicitly be encouraged

● to question and show curiosity;

● to find out rather than use preconceived ideas;

● to take note of all the evidence in developing and testing their ideas;

● to be critical of their own ideas and ways of working;

● to realise that they can learn through their own activity and gradually to take on responsibility for their learning.

What we have in these three lists are the ideas or concepts of science, the science process skills, and the attitudes to science. Spelling them out in this way may help to show what learning we are aiming

for, and that this learning is closely related both to common sense and to the aims of other areas of the curriculum. The aims can of course be specified more precisely and we shall need to do this later (see Chapters 8 and 10).

Learning in and out of school

Children don't only explore, investigate, solve problems and form ideas in school; they do these all the time. They will learn about things in the world around them even if science isn't included in the school curriculum. So why is it necessary? An answer is to be found in some of the 'everyday' ideas that children have which seem rather strange and unscientific: that switching on a light in a darkened room is like switching on your eyes; that slugs are snails which have parked their shells; that things which are small and light float on water regardless of what they are made of; that things which dissolve in water disappear entirely. All of these ideas are reasonable first ideas which children will form from limited observations. It is when these ideas persist and are not modified or replaced by more helpful ones that children encounter difficulties in developing their understanding of their surroundings. Scientific activities at school can help in the way ideas are formed, or existing ideas tested and changed in the light of evidence, so that children are not left with their 'everyday' ideas unchallenged.

Just how this is done cannot be put in a sentence. As with all learning, the starting point is where the learners are, so it is important to be able to recognise this and to provide children with the appropriate challenges and opportunities for advancement. We shall give some help with this in a later chapter; but the starting point for the teacher is the first thing to consider. There may not be as much of the kind of science that we've described here as we might hope to see in the primary classroom. So the next chapter gives some ideas for how to start making changes.

STARTING POINTS

Lack of confidence in ability to teach science effectively is widespread among primary teachers. Research (e.g. Wragg *et al.*, 1989; Harlen *et al.*, 1995) has shown that primary teachers rate their confidence in teaching science below that for all other subjects except music, design technology and information technology.

The aspects of science seen as a cause of most anxiety are consistently found to be the provision, organisation and use of equipment, responding to questions that seem to demand subject knowledge, and the assessment and recording of progress. Many teachers cope with these difficulties by confining investigative work to that using only the simplest and safest equipment (from the point of view of whether 'it will work'), using prescriptive work cards or sheets, and avoiding situations where awkward questions might arise. In doing so, of course, the children's opportunities for learning many of the ideas, skills and attitudes that we touched upon in the last chapter are lost.

Where do we start?

Many teachers share feelings that science is a difficult subject because it appears to require specialist knowledge, and that it makes organisational demands which seem daunting, given all the pressures of work in primary school. Whilst not wishing to minimise the reality of such concerns for some teachers, it is important to realise that, although these anxieties are real, they can be overcome. For a start the potential for science already exists in normal primary practices. For example:

- all classrooms, however cramped, contain a range of everyday materials that are used for various purposes;

- all children handle materials in the course of their normal work;

- all teachers talk with children about their work.

The two essential commodities, *materials* and *talk*, are present in every classroom; making changes towards active enquiry-based science is a matter of being prepared to explore and exploit them to engage children in practical investigations and problem-solving.

For teachers, the practical implications of this are gaining experience of:

- the particular ways in which materials can be explored by children in order to promote scientific activity;

- the kind of classroom talk that can stimulate and structure children's scientific experience.

The key ingredient for implementation is the willingness of teachers to become involved and to gain confidence through success. What follows is selected to do just that.

How do we start?

We will start with a problem: *which fabric is best for keeping us dry?* This is a good problem for scientific investigation by children of all ages. There is a variety of ways in which it might be introduced:

- semi-spontaneously, where preference is for responding to the immediacy of topical interests, for example when there is a sudden interest-capturing downpour in a spell of dry weather when many children have come to school without rainy-day clothes, or, perhaps, when someone has come to school resplendent in a new raincoat that invites comment;

- pre-planned, as an activity within a wider topic, for example weather, or clothes and clothing;

- deliberately, in a 'today we are going to be scientists' style; an approach that works well with juniors;

- indirectly, as a challenge that might be presented as part of a display on, say, materials, or it can be effective presented on its own, as a new classroom event with novelty appeal.

No matter how the problem is introduced, the activity that follows will need planning in terms of resources, a teaching sequence and class organisation.

Resources

Essentially children will require the following.

1. *Some fabrics:*

- ideally, acquire some old clothes from a jumble sale (or ask children to bring in old clothes or scraps of cloth);

- more conveniently, raid the school fabric box.

Whatever the source, it's useful to limit the range of fabrics available during the activity. Three or four different kinds are usually all that children new to this work can cope with. It's not necessary to name the fabrics (though some teachers might feel happier to select those known to them should the children ask).

Do some private investigation to decide the best selection of fabrics: try dropping water on them. Include in your selection one that water goes through fairly readily and one, e.g. felt, on which a drop of water forms a ball on the surface and is only slowly absorbed. It's a good idea to avoid fabrics that children know to be waterproof, otherwise any investigation may seem pointless to them and they are likely to respond in a 'this one's best – so what?' manner. The approach could be along the lines 'If these are all we have, which would keep us driest?'.

2. *Some means of simulating rain:*

- courageously, use toy watering cans;

- less dramatically, use any container that the children can manipulate competently for pouring. With potential spillage in mind it's sensible to keep the containers as small as is conveniently possible (old film-spool containers, for instance).

3. *Some means of seeing what happens when water falls on the fabrics:*

- it is important to respond to, and let the children try out, any ideas they have (such as placing the fabric on their hand and feeling if water comes through); but

- should ideas not be forthcoming, then 'stage-manage' the situation. For example, use the approach 'Should we try this?' and, with them, place the fabric over a see-through container (plastic party glasses are good) and hold it in place with an elastic band, or use a less direct approach 'Perhaps these would help' and simply supply the equipment.

A teaching sequence

Having sorted out the kind of resources needed, it is now necessary to have a teaching sequence in mind before sorting out the thorny problem of class organisation. The activity will fall into four phases:

- setting up the problem;

- preliminary exploration;

- investigating;

- concluding discussion.

Setting up the problem

This is a short verbal session with three phases of development.

1. *Make sure that the problem has meaning for the children in terms of their own experience.* Some teachers might favour an initial focus on the clothes the children are wearing using a speculative approach of the kind:

'If we were out without coats and it poured with rain, whose jumper/sweater would be best for keeping you dry?'

The question will promote useful talk.

2. *Develop the meaning phase with a focus on the actual materials to be tested* via a question of the kind 'Which of these would be best?'. Ask for the children's ideas and reasons for choosing one or another.

3. *Establish that practical action is needed to put opinions to the test.* Most likely there will be a range of opinions in a group and the situation can be structured to favour activity via 'I wonder who's right? What could we do to find out?'. Should there already be unanimous agreement on which would be best then suggest 'What could we do to find out if we're right?'.

Preliminary exploration

In this phase children will be exploring what happens when water falls on the different fabrics and it is important that they do this in their own terms. They are likely to be fascinated by specific events, such as the 'balling' of water on felt, and in responding to such particular happenings they may well lose sight of the original problem. What happens may lead some to explore tangentially, dropping water on other things; some may carry out repetitive drop-making, exploring big drops and little drops. Few, if any, are likely to work systematically in an attack on the problem. This is usual for children inexperienced in scientific investigation and is, in fact, a diagnostic indication of the level of investigative skills. For this reason the preliminary exploration should not be rushed, nor should it be over-structured by teachers anxious to move quickly towards 'getting an answer'.

For some children this exploratory phase may well be sufficient as an early scientific experience, but it is useful to help them draw together what they have done and encourage comparison between the fabrics by asking 'What happens when ...?'. They might classify the fabrics as good/not good for keeping water out, or put them in rank order of best → worst.

Once comparisons have been made the scene is set for the next phase, of investigating.

Investigating

The key idea here is that of the 'fair test'. When children say that one fabric is better than another for keeping rain out, have they been fair to the fabrics in their testing? What might have made their comparison unfair? It is important to find out the children's ideas on the subject. Probably someone will identify that to be fair they need to use the same amount of water on each fabric, though this will not necessarily happen. Lack of response is another indication of the level of the children's investigative skills. It might also be that the whole idea of fairness in this situation is so new to them that they are not sure what response is wanted, so it's a good idea to probe with questions of the kind 'Does it matter how much water we use?'.

Work towards suggestions from the children of how to treat the fabrics in a fair way and then let them carry out their test, or repeat it if necessary, using their ideas.

Look for opportunities to focus the work towards measurement, for example, 'How much better is this fabric than that for keeping out the rain?' but beware of moving too quickly in this direction. Most children will not be ready for precision work until they have had a considerable amount of experience in general comparative testing.

Concluding discussion

It is likely that there is no obvious end to the activity since children often have more and more ideas about what they can do as they gain confidence in their own ability to find things out. But it is important to make time for a whole group or class discussion before the time for the activity runs out. Bring the children together to describe to each other briefly what they did and, particularly, what was the evidence they used to decide which fabric was best. How did what they found agree with their initial ideas about which would be best? If there was a difference, what do they think might be the reason? Did they think their tests were fair? If they were to do this again, how might they change what they did?

Talking about the work is a legitimate form of communication (see page 17) and need not necessarily be followed by 'writing it up'. If children are just starting out on investigative work, discussion, guided by questions from the teacher, helps them to know what to pay attention to and what is significant to report. When children are used to sharing their experiences in this way, they will be in a better position to structure what they write about their work when it's appropriate to make a more permanent record.

Class organisation

Let's now consider ways of organising the practical work of testing the fabrics. There are many possibilities, but they fall into three kinds:

(a) one group only involved in science; the rest engaged in other activities less demanding of teacher attention;
(b) the whole class, divided into smallish groups, each involved in similar science work;
(c) the whole class, divided into smallish groups, each involved in different kinds of science work.

There is a further way that is useful when either or both the teacher and children are new to active investigative work, which is to start in out-of-class time if this is possible within the school. This enables a start to be made without having to cope with organisational pressures. Many teachers have gained confidence in the approach by undertaking the work with children in a science or general interest club; this has the obvious advantage of allowing ideas to be tried out with well-motivated children. Later, as confidence grows, investigative work is drawn into class time.

(a) *One group only on science*

Starting with a group of five or six children gives the teacher chance to focus more clearly on the science. The rest of the class need to be doing

work that is not too dependent on the teacher, which can pose a difficulty. With a class unused to practical group activity some teachers have:

● set the other children writing/reading tasks and handled their natural interest in the work of the practical group with the response 'Your turn will come';

● adopted a similar approach but with the rest of the class doing art and craft work, for which the necessary techniques have been taught, in which case all the children are involved in some kind of practical work. This probably creates different kinds of demand, but not less demand on the teacher's attention.

To give all groups a turn at practical science work is clearly difficult in this kind of organisation, and may mean that for large periods of time the children not involved in science are being 'kept busy'. Furthermore, the discussion at the end of the activity involves only one group, so that sharing of ideas across the class is limited. So this may be a useful way of starting, rather than a more permanent regime.

(b) *The whole class, in groups, on the same science work*

This makes heavy resource demands, and it can be difficult to give detailed attention to any one group. Nevertheless, there are also advantages. If the problem has been well set up, the children do not need attention all of the time – indeed it is a positive advantage for them to be left alone to do their own thinking whilst the teacher is busy elsewhere – and the teacher is having to deal with only one type of activity at a time and is not continually jumping from one to another. Moreover, the final discussion comes at the time when the investigations are fresh in the minds of all the children.

(c) *The whole class, in groups, on different kinds of science work*

In the case of the work on fabrics one group might be doing the practical testing whilst others do work of a non-practical nature, either making a record of their exploratory work or using books to gain information about fabrics. In other cases, where demands on equipment may be greater, staggering the practical work may be a necessity. But the whole-class discussion can still be held at a time when all children will have reached a certain point in the work.

As we see, there are pros and cons for each form of organisation; there are no 'golden rules' and no best patterns for organising the work. Each teacher will have to find his or her own preferred working patterns, keeping in mind that the more opportunity there is for constructively interacting with the children as they work, the more productive the work is likely to be.

Applying the approach

In whatever way the practical work is organised,

the guidelines in Fig. 2.1 summarise the steps in this approach to making a start. In particular, the key questions that help structure children's activity are likely to prove useful.

The same approach can be used with different materials. Here are some more problems which will extend the children's experience:

- which fabric is best for keeping the wind out? (a development of the interest in fabrics);

- which kind of paper is best for covering a book? (a more complex problem that might be developed through an interest in testing);

- which kind of paper towel is best for soaking up water? (a problem readily introduced when water has to be mopped up!)

Be prepared

Things may not go as expected and problems may arise, so it is as well to be prepared to

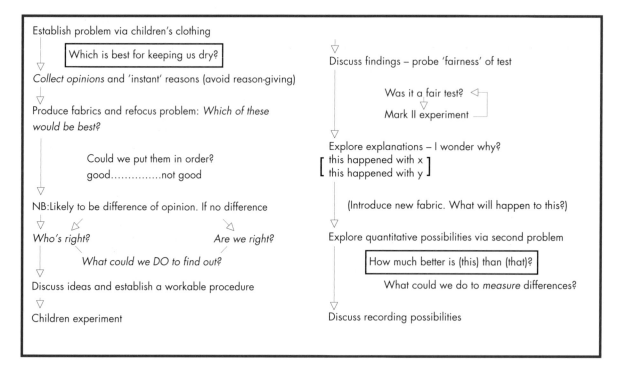

Fig. 2.1 Steps in the approach

Problem and possible reasons	Response
Ideas are not forthcoming from the children. They may be uncertain of what is expected of them in a new style of working	Show that the children's ideas are valued, whatever these are. Be patient, give more experience of exploring materials and sharing ideas
The children find it difficult to sustain interest. Sometimes the desire of teachers to keep the children moving on through the task may take the children out of one phase before they've had sufficient time to gain confidence in working with materials	Give more time for the free exploration of materials. Don't be anxious to turn this into systematic activity. Stop when interest flags and return to the materials later
The children have difficulty with the idea of a fair test. This is an indication that they need a lot more activity with materials	Let them work with the materials in their own way, and probe, in discussion, what they think they have found
The children have difficulty working cooperatively. Even children well used to group working in other areas of the curriculum are likely to have initial problems when they handle and share materials in an investigative manner	Give gentle reminders. Give reasons for the need to cooperate in terms of the scientific activity ('scientists find out more by working with each other' type of approach)
The children ask questions the teacher cannot answer. This happens to even the most experienced and knowledgeable teacher. It can never be avoided as long as children are inquisitive, as they should be, about the things they find around them	Pages 18 and 19 give some approaches to this problem. Take heart in the knowledge that children's questions tend to change, as they gain more experience in investigative work and learn from the teacher's example, from emphasis on information to questions that can be answered by enquiry

Table 2.1 Possible problems and useful responses

deal with what may happen. Table 2.1 summarises some often-encountered problems with possible reasons for them and what to do in response. These may help teachers to anticipate and avert difficulties that might otherwise reduce confidence. More is said about tackling difficulties in the next chapter.

After having 'had a go' at the fabric activities with some or all of the class, it is a good idea to take a little time to sit back and reflect on what the children were doing and to consider, as an on-looker might, the part the teacher was taking. This is a good thing to do in any situation, for if we are always close to the action and solving moment-to-moment problems of keeping things going, there is a tendency to lose sight of longer-term objectives. It is especially important when trying something new, however, to ask oneself the question 'Am I on the right lines?'. Attempting to answer this question should help to identify, at an early stage, whether or not changes in approach and organisation are needed.

Reviewing the children's activities

We look first at what the children were doing. Think back over the fabric-testing activities and reflect on the questions in the checklists which follow. Note that the questions are expressed in general terms so that they can be used in relation to other activities as well as to the fabric activity, and so the more general word 'materials' is used to include a range of objects and articles that children might investigate. (It is unfortunate that fabrics are loosely called materials!)

Checklists

In the preliminary exploration phase

- Were the children handling materials themselves?

- Did they observe the materials closely – perhaps smelling, feeling, listening, as well as looking?

- Did they try things 'to see what happens'?

- Did they group some things together according to what they had found out?

- Did they use their observations to put things in an order?

- Did they discuss with each other what they were doing?

- Did they compare what they found with what others found?

- Did they discuss their work with you?

- Did they ask questions or puzzle over anything they found?

- Were they kept busy and absorbed by what they were doing?

- Did they base their statements on evidence rather than preconceived ideas?

In the investigating phase

- Did the children have a clear idea of what they were trying to find out or compare?

- Did they devise a test which was relevant to what they wanted to find out?

- Did they consider how to carry out the test in a fair manner?

- Did they actually control variables to make the test fair when they carried it out?

- Did they use instruments to aid their observation or for taking measurements?

- Did they obtain and use quantitative results (not just 'more than' but 'how much more than')?

- Did they make a record of what they did or of their results?

- Did they discuss their results with each other?
- Did they look for evidence to support their statements?
- Were any conclusions reached consistent with their results?
- Did they check or repeat parts of their investigation?
- Did they try different approaches to a problem?

In the concluding discussion

- Did all the children take part?
- Did they criticise what they had done and identify ways of improving their investigation?
- Did they compare what they found with what they initially expected?
- Did they try to explain their findings, for example, why one material turned out to be best?

Implications of the answers

The questions in the checklists are expressed in a way which make it obvious that the best answer is 'yes' to all of them. They indicate some of the things that it is suggested children ought to be doing in science activities. There are good reasons for suggesting these things, for they give children opportunities to develop the ideas, skills and attitudes which were mentioned briefly in Chapter 1 (pages 3 and 4). Later, in Chapter 4, we will discuss further the justification for the suggestions implied in the lists. For the moment we turn to the implications of the answers to the questions.

There is no problem in cases where the answer to the question is a clear 'yes'. But where there is doubt, or an honest answer is 'no', then some further reflection is necessary. 'No' answers to the 'preliminary exploration' list are particularly worth studying, for they might indicate that the children were not really engaged in fruitful interaction with the materials. If there are more than one or two 'no' answers here, it is necessary to recall what the

children were doing instead of the things in the list. Were they:

- ignoring materials given?
- disputing possession of the materials?
- looking only superficially at the materials?
- spending most of their time writing or drawing?
- just watching others and not joining in?
- using materials in unintended ways?
- moving around the classroom, fetching and carrying materials?
- talking about things not related to the task in hand?
- doing anything else?

Answering 'yes' to some of these questions could indicate that more attention might need to be given to how the problem was set up. Some possible sources of difficulties include:

- perhaps not enough materials were provided;
- perhaps the children's interest in the particular materials had not been sufficiently awakened;
- perhaps they did not understand what they were supposed to be doing;
- perhaps they needed more help to realise that they can find things out for themselves through their own actions;
- perhaps they view school work as being essentially a matter of writing.

Suggestions given on page 15 may help where these difficulties apply.

In the 'investigating' phase, 'no' answers to several questions in the checklist are perhaps to be expected, certainly at the start. Some items on the list (e.g. checking and repeating parts of an investigation) refer to things that it is known children tend not to do when left to themselves. Others (e.g. using measuring instruments and collecting quantitative results) are more relevant to certain problems than to others where qualitative results are entirely adequate. Indeed, all the items in this list indicate more advanced levels of skills and attitudes than is the case for the 'preliminary exploration' list.

Although a full set of 'yes' answers is not expected at the start, it is, of course, necessary to think about what can be done to work towards advancing children's investigative abilities. This is something we will take up later, in Chapters 7 and 8, where we discuss how to assess children's progress in particular ideas, skills and attitudes, and consider ways of helping this progress. For the moment, however, our focus is at a more general level, remembering that we want children to:

- think for themselves about their investigations;

- do the investigations for themselves;

- work out for themselves what their results mean;

- review and improve for themselves what they have done.

The emphasis on thinking as well as doing brings us to the importance of the 'discussion' phase. Genuine discussion should enable the participants to respond to each other on an equal footing. Its role in the context of investigative work is that it provides both: a vehicle for teachers to encourage children to think aloud, to do their own thinking (and to realise that they can indeed do this) and not depend on instructions from others; and a channel for children to reflect critically on their work, in terms of how well results are backed up by evidence and how procedures could have been improved.

If, then, there is a high proportion of 'no' answers to the questions in the list for the 'concluding discussion', it may be that:

- the children are not used to sharing their ideas and work in this way;

- the children need much more practice in relating ideas to evidence

- someone (the teacher or a child) was dominating the talking, giving others little invitation to take part;

- the questions used to start were too focused and gave no encouragement for a range of different answers;

- the investigation had not engaged the children (that is, there were a number of 'no' answers even for the 'preliminary exploration').

As the concluding discussion is dependent on what went on before, improving the interaction with the materials and with the problem will set the scene for more fruitful discussion. However, the extent to which children feel able to share their ideas, whatever they are, depends crucially on the kind of questions the teacher asks. It will be enormously helped by teachers asking open questions and ones expressing interest in children's ideas ('What do *you* think about . . .').

The importance of time

Chapter 2 mentioned 'materials' and 'talk' as key starting points for science. We now add *time* as a key factor in giving opportunity for advancing children's learning. Anyone who has tried the approach proposed will realise that it takes more time than a conventional lesson where children are told what to do or just given information to memorise.

The time needed for children to do things for themselves is always much greater than if other people do them for the children. This applies to thinking as much as to tying shoe laces. But, as with tying shoe laces, children will never learn to think for themselves if someone else always does the thinking for them. So we must expect that deciding what to do, working it out in practice and then doing it will take children longer – perhaps two or three times longer – than following instructions which tell them what to do. But in this time they will be learning much more science in one activity which is thought through, than if they filled the same time doing several activities in which they didn't have to think for themselves.

Reviewing the teacher's activities

In responding to reflection on what the children were or were not doing, we have already indicated actions for the teacher to consider taking. In looking more directly at the teacher's role, we first list some questions which help to diagnose the actions it might be necessary to take and then propose ways of dealing with the aspects which initially present difficulties to many teachers.

A checklist for self-diagnosis

Reflecting on their own part in the activities, teachers should ask themselves, did they:

- provide enough materials of the right kind?
- provide time and opportunity for children to explore and play with the materials informally before engaging in more systematic investigation?
- encourage children to ask questions?
- respond to questions that the children asked by suggesting what the children might do to find out rather than providing a direct answer?
- ask open questions and ones that encouraged children to talk about their ideas?
- set up the group tasks so that the children knew that they were expected to investigate and to use their own ideas?
- notice children engaged in their activity, working well without help?
- deliberately keep silent at times to listen to the children talking?
- become aware of the children's ideas about the materials being studied?
- notice any change in the children's ideas?
- discuss with them the evidence on which they were basing their conclusions?

There are also other aspects of the teacher's role which we have not discussed yet but which should also be part of a teacher's regular reflection on his or her role. These include assessing and recording the children's progress in their developing skills, ideas and attitudes; these will be taken up in Chapters 7, 8, and 9. So, for the sake of completeness, we should add to the self-assessment list a further four questions for teachers to ask themselves. Did they:

- keep records of the children's experiences?
- gather information to help assess the children's ideas and skills?
- use their assessment of the children's progress in planning further activities?
- talk to the children about the progress they were making and encourage them to assess their own work?

Suggestions for tackling likely areas of difficulty

Engaging children's interest in the problem as a real one

Setting the scene is important here, as is timing. For some topics it is useful to mount a display of relevant objects in the classroom. Encourage the children to touch and talk about the objects and add some of their own. Add something each day prior to starting a class discussion. In the case of the waterproof fabrics, the weather will probably oblige with a convenient downpour. Start the discussion by referring to this and to the appearance of anyone coming into the school showing signs of having been in the rain.

Transferring the children's interest from the general problem to one which can be tackled with the materials provided

Spend more time on general discussion before

'homing in' on the problem. With the raincoats, for example, have a parade of rainwear; divide the articles into groups according to features noticed by the children; regroup by different criteria; choose two very similar coats and list the differences; choose two very different ones and list the similarities. Which is most waterproof? (We don't know.) Could we find out? (Better not to experiment on the coats.) Let's see if we can decide this question for these pieces of fabric . . . .

Encouraging children to 'have a go' rather than ask for answers

Some children need an invitation to start interacting with the materials, before a specific problem is posed. So the question 'Can you find out which is best . . . ?' or 'How can you test . . . ?' may be too far ahead of these children. Instead, try comparison questions such as 'In what ways are they the same? In what ways do they differ?' and 'What happens if . . . ?' first.

Responding to unexpected things that children do

If we want children to use their own ideas we shouldn't be surprised, but pleased, when they do something unexpected. However, there's no doubt that it can be disconcerting, for instance, to find the children sewing the fabrics instead of testing them with water! Unless something dangerous is likely to happen, though, stop yourself 'jumping in' straight away. Observe carefully from a slight distance so that you know just what is happening and then ask the children to explain to you their view of what they are doing and what they are hoping to achieve through it. It is likely that they have a good reason – good in their minds – for what they are doing or, if not, in telling you about it they will probably realise their mistaken reasoning. (The children in question thought that if the fabrics they were given were too tough to sew or would tear at the seams, they'd be no good for a raincoat anyway!)

Supplying additional materials requested by the children for their explorations

With experience it becomes easier to anticipate children's need for containers, sticks, cardboard, pieces of tubing, etc. Many teachers find it helpful, as well as being useful to the children, to ask them to plan ahead what they will need and to write it down during one session of science in preparation for the next session.

Judging when to bring this phase of the activity to a close

Let the children help, indirectly, in judging the point for rounding off an activity, or a phase of it. If the activity appears to be waning, or losing focus, give the children a few minutes' warning to prepare an oral or written account for you of what they have done. This account will help in judging whether they have already done as much as could be expected or whether they have not really come to grips with the problem. The appropriate action can then be taken.

Ensuring equal participation of all children in a group

Where there is a problem of ensuring equal participation in the activity among the members of a group, it is sometimes necessary to discuss the problem with them. Help them to agree to defining tasks within the activity and to a fair system of taking turns at those tasks. If the problem persists it may be necessary to experiment with changes in group membership.

Encouraging children to make some appropriate record of their work

It is helpful to think of any record the children make of their work in the context of their whole communication about the activity. Discussion, notes, drawings, models, paintings and a display of work are all parts of this communication and each has a different role to play. There is nothing special about written work and it should not be asked for as a ritual. Thus, at times, particularly in the early stages of 'getting going' in science, it may not be necessary to make a record. Instead there should be plenty of talk to help children review and reflect upon what they have done.

At the same time, however, writing does have a particularly efficient function in communication and we want children to become used to and proficient in using it. Among written forms of communication there are both personal notes and public reports to consider. Personal notes are necessary to assist in planning, to record things that may be forgotten and for taking down results. A long-term aim is to encourage children to use notebooks to jot down, for themselves, notes, drawings, measurements, which will help their investigation. These are not the kind of record that people usually mean when they talk about recording work, but they are a very important part of the activity.

It is the public report, the kind that emerges only at the end of an activity, which is usually of more concern to teachers. It is much less of a problem, however, when it is seen by both teacher and children to be relevant and appropriate. Relevance comes from having some function, which is usually that of telling others about what has been done. So it is necessary for the record to be seen to be used for that purpose; not just pinned on the wall (if it is on paper) but talked about by those who produced it; not an isolated artefact but one which the makers explain, demonstrate and show how they solved practical problems in its construction.

Appropriateness has a double significance in this context:

- what is appropriate for the children at their stage in active learning;

- what is the best medium for the particular information to be communicated.

It may be a chart, a graph, a model, etc., and it may only need a few words of explanation or invitation to a potential audience. As children's work becomes more sophisticated, they themselves will find that it needs more words of explanation and then some structure in reporting will be appropriate, but this should not be introduced prematurely.

Bringing the activity to a conclusion

The making and communication of a record is one part of bringing the activity to a conclusion. It is best seen in the context of exchanging reports from different groups and giving all children the chance to see the work of the class brought together and to comment on it. Children are always interested in what other groups have been doing, especially if there is a linking theme but they have not been doing the same as each other. It is useful to establish that a whole-class discussion will generally be held at the end of a topic, and that groups will be expected to show and describe their work and findings. Preparing for this brings relevance to the children's reporting and makes them consider an appropriate form for the communication. It also ensures that work is rounded off by the group, not stopped in mid-investigation, and it makes them review for themselves what they have done in preparation for describing it to others. Sometimes the combined reports and products can be put together in a display in some public area of the school for other classes, parents and visitors to see.

Answering the children's questions

Handling questions depends on the type of question, so it is difficult to sum up at a general level in a few words. The following extract should help.

Handling children's questions

(From S. Jelly, 'Helping children raise questions – and answering them', in *Primary Science: Taking the Plunge*, 1985, pp. 53–6.)

Spontaneous questions from children come in various forms and carry a variety of meanings. Consider for example the following questions. How would you respond to each?

1. What is a baby tiger called?
2. What makes it rain?
3. Why can you see yourself in a window?
4. Why is the hamster ill?
5. If I mix these (paints), what colour will I get?
6. If God made the world, who made God?
7. How long do cows live?
8. How does a computer work?
9. When will the tadpoles be frogs?
10. Are there people in outer space?

Clearly the nature of each question shapes our response to it. Even assuming we wanted to give children the correct answers, we could not do so in all cases. Question 6 has no answer, but we can of course respond to it. Question 10 is similar; it has no certain answer but we could provide a conjectural one based on some relevant evidence. All the other questions do have answers, but this does not mean that each answer is similar in kind, nor does it mean that all answers are known to the teacher, nor are all answers equally accessible to children.

When we analyse what we do everyday as part of our stock-in-trade, namely respond to children's questions, we encounter a highly complex situation. Not only do questions vary in kind, requiring answers that differ in kind, but children also have different reasons for asking a question. The question may mean 'I want a direct answer', it might mean 'I've asked the question to show you I'm interested but I'm not after a literal answer'. Or, it could mean, 'I've asked the question because I want your attention – the answer is not important'. Given all these variables how then should we handle the questions raised spontaneously in science work? The comment of one teacher is pertinent here:

> 'The children's questions worry me. I can deal with the child who just wants attention, but because I've no science background I take other questions at face value and get bothered when I don't know the answer. I don't mind saying I don't know, though I don't want to do it too often. I've tried the 'let's find out together' approach, but it's not easy and can be very frustrating.'

Many teachers will identify with these remarks and what follows is a suggested strategy for those in a similar position. It's not the only strategy possible, nor is it completely fail safe, but it has helped a large number of teachers deal with difficult questions. By difficult questions I mean those that require complex information and/or explanation for a full answer. The approach does not apply to simple informational questions such as 1, 7 and 9 on the list above because these are easy to handle, either by telling or by reference to books, or expertise, in ways familiar to the children in other subject areas. Nor is it relevant to spontaneous questions of the productive kind discussed earlier, because these can be answered by doing. Essentially it is a strategy for handling complex questions and in particular those of the 'why' kind that are the most frequent of all spontaneous questions. They are difficult questions because they carry an apparent request for a full explanation which may not be known to the teacher and, in any case, is likely to be conceptionally beyond a child's understanding.

The strategy recommended is one that turns the question to practical action with a 'let's see what we can do to understand more' approach.

The teacher skill involved is the ability to 'turn' the question. Consider, for example, a situation in which children are exploring the properties of fabrics. They have dropped water on different types and become fascinated by the fact that water stays 'like a little ball' on felt. They tilt the felt, rolling the ball around, and someone asks 'Why is it like a ball?'. How might the question be turned by applying the 'doing more to understand' approach? We need to analyse the situation quickly and use what I call a 'variables scan'. The explanation must relate to something 'going on' between the water and the felt surface so causing the ball. That being so, ideas for children's activities will come if we consider ways in which the situation could be varied to better understand the making of the ball. We could explore surfaces keeping the drop the same, and explore drops keeping the surface the same. These thoughts can prompt others that bring ideas nearer to what children might do. For example:

1. Focusing on the surface, keeping the drop the same:
    What is special about the felt that helps make the ball?
    Which fabrics are good 'ball-makers'? Which are poor?
    What have the good ball-making fabrics in common?
    What surfaces are good 'ball-makers'? Which are poor?
    What properties do these share with the good ball-making fabrics?
    Can we turn the felt into a poor ball-maker?

2. Focusing on the water drop, keeping the surface the same:
    Are all fluids good ball-makers?
    Can we turn the water into a poor ball-maker?

Notice how the 'variables scan' results in the development of productive questions that can be explored by the children. The original question has been turned to practical activity and children exploring along these lines will certainly enlarge their understanding of which is involved in the phenomenon. They will not arrive at a detailed explanation but may be led towards simple generalization of their experience, such as 'A ball will form when ...' or 'It will not form when ...'.

Some teachers see the strategy as one of diversion (which it is) and are uneasy that the original question remains unanswered, but does this matter? The question has promoted worthwhile scientific enquiry and we must remember that its meaning for the child may well have been 'I'm asking it to communicate my interest'. For such children interest has certainly been developed, and children who may have initiated the question as a request for explanation, in practice, are normally satisfied by the work their question generates.

The strategy can be summarized as follows:

Analyse the question

↓

Consider if it can be 'turned' to practical activity (with its 'real' materials or by simulating them)

↓

Carry out a 'variables scan' and identify productive questions

↓

Use questions to promote activity

↓

Consider simple generalization children might make *from experience*

4

WHY THIS WAY OF WORKING?

- *Why is it worthwhile making the effort to teach science in the ways suggested in the past two chapters?*

- *Isn't it enough to have, for instance, a good display, some demonstrations and some posters and let the children get the rest from books?*

- *Why all the stress on providing materials for children to do things with?*

- *Why not let them follow instructions, so that they get things right?*

- *Where is this way of working leading us?*

Some of these questions may well have come to mind when initiating practical enquiry-based science. Some convincing answers are needed, which not only answer critics but also provide a sound basis for present and future decisions about science work in the class and throughout the school.

This chapter is about the rationale for working in the way proposed in this book. We believe the purposes are sound, but they are not necessarily simple. Teachers who feel their priority is to get on with the 'doing', may not wish to do more than skim this chapter on first reading and spend more time trying the activities suggested in other chapters. But it is important to come back to it later, because understanding the learning that this approach tries to nurture in children is a necessary basis for development of the practical aspects of the work. Teachers can more easily create and use ideas of their own, once they know where they are going!

How are classroom decisions made?

Think for a moment about planning activities in some other area of the curriculum, say physical education. What influences the decision to choose certain activities rather than others, how to organise the children (in teams, groups or individually), whether or not to use certain equipment, whether to encourage or discourage competition? The answers probably make reference to shortage of resources or space, but beyond that, where there is a real choice, they no doubt reflect what the teacher wants children to learn and how he or she thinks that learning is best brought about, for certain children, at a particular time.

Making decisions in science is no different; we base them on what we think is worthwhile learning in science. Let's take some of the ways in which science lessons could be conducted:

- teacher demonstration to the whole class;

- TV programmes;

- working from books;

- working with materials individually;

- working with materials in groups;

- any other way you can think of.

Now consider to what extent each of these gives opportunities for children to:

(a) gather evidence at first hand by direct observation;
(b) use their own ideas in making sense of new experiences;
(c) explore and test materials;
(d) learn about others' ideas;
(e) make and test predictions based on their own and others' ideas;
(f) improve their ways of exploring, investigating and making sense of things around them.

It soon becomes apparent that certain kinds of provision preclude certain kinds of learning experience. If we value these learning experiences then we have to organise provision that is consistent with them.

Similar points could be made about the role of the teacher. For instance, which of (a) to (f) above are encouraged if the teacher takes the role of:

- provider of expert knowledge?

- fellow enquirer?

- technician and source of material?

This important relationship between classroom decisions and learning opportunities has two implications:

- what we decide to provide and how we organise it constrains the kind of learning that can take place; and, conversely,

- how we view learning will influence what opportunities we provide.

Let's look at these implications a little more closely.

Decision-making framework

Although we perhaps don't consciously carry out planning as a sequence of steps, starting with nothing except ideas, it's useful to think of the classroom situation as being a result of deciding what learning opportunities we want to provide; and these in turn are a result of having in mind a certain view of what kind of learning is desirable. In other words:

1. We start with an idea about the *kind of learning* we want to bring about (e.g. whether we want learning with understanding or some other kind of learning).

2. Then we decide the *learning experiences* which we think will be likely to give opportunities for this kind of learning.

3. Next we arrange for these learning experiences to take place; this involves thinking about *materials, the roles of teacher and pupils* in interacting with them, and *the necessary organisation*.

4. Finally, we decide how to *evaluate* how successful we have been.

Of course all of these decisions are made within a variety of constraints (limitations of money, time, energy and our own professional expertise). We never reach the position of being entirely satisfied with what we are doing and we should always keep it under review. Chapter 3 has given some ideas for reviewing the provision of activities aimed at improving the kind of learning we value. Chapters 7 and 8 suggest how we may find out whether the learning is taking place.

The four points listed above describe decision-making in a way which applies to any teaching that is internally consistent and well planned, whatever the type of learning embraced. It applies equally to rote learning, as it does to more progressive ways of learning. For example, take the teacher who was asked why she arranged her class with desks all facing the front, in rows, forbade the children to talk to each other and occupied them mainly in copying from the blackboard. She replied: 'Because that's the way they learn; from me and the blackboard, not by talking to each other'. However much we may disagree with her view, we must admit that her organisation and the experiences she provided were consistent with it!

Our purpose here is not to justify rote learning! The example has been given only to emphasise that classroom decisions determine the kind of learning that children can experience. Therefore to show where we are going through the sorts of classroom activities we have been discussing and trying, it is necessary to think about children's learning.

Learning as changing ideas

Observations of children tackling new problems show the importance of making links between what is already known and what is new. Children faced with a new object or material invariably make statements or ask questions which show the struggle to make sense of the new in terms of existing ideas:

'I think it's ...' or 'Look, it's just like ...' are typical first reactions.

Similarly, adults search around to relate a new object or event to something encountered previously. For example:

> Imagine being handed a type of fungus that you have never seen before. By looking at certain features you would soon recognise it as a natural rather than a human-made object and you might even be able to link experience of other fungi to suggest at least the sort of organism that it is.

When such previous learning is absent, we experience the feeling of not being able to make sense of something new – for instance, our first encounter with a computer! Then we, like children, need to build up understanding bit by bit, starting with something which does make sense to us and then linking in each new step to existing knowledge.

Children, then, don't develop ideas from scratch about a new event or object; learning begins by linking existing ideas to it and using them in an attempt to understand it. The ideas which are linked need to be checked to see if they are useful, and if they fit further experience.

The linking process involves the skills of:

● observing;

● raising questions;

● hypothesising (attempting to explain);

and the checking processes involve the skills of:

● predicting;

● investigating;

● interpreting;

● communicating.

These skills are called *science process skills*. In addition, practical activities are likely, as suggested in Chapter 1, to give the opportunity for learning in technology as well as in science using the technological skills of designing, making and evaluating. However, whilst recognising the close connection with technology, our focus here will be on the science skills. Many of these are used in enquiry-based work across the curriculum, but it is the practical testing and investigation that distinguishes science from other areas of the curriculum. Other subject areas also use observation, hypothesising, communication, etc., but practical checking of predictions by changing some things and not others is particular to science. These checking processes are of special importance in children's experience of scientific activity.

The process of checking may show that the idea which has been linked is helpful, or it may show that it is not, or that it could be helpful if modified. So an idea always emerges changed in some way from being applied and tested. It may be changed by being reinforced and shown to be helpful in understanding the new situation, or by being modified in some way in order to be helpful. Even an idea that is rejected is changed by having been shown not to be applicable in the new context. How the changed ideas are useful in future learning depends on the initial ideas the children have access to and on the way in which the 'processing' is done. We will consider each of these in turn.

Children's existing ideas

These are a mixture of partially formed scientific ideas, probably already changed by experience, and ideas we might call 'everyday' rather than scientific, since they have very limited value in helping understanding. There are plenty of 'everyday' ideas around for children to pick up, from the media (especially advertisements, e.g. 'Nothing tastes better than butter!') and other parts of daily life. Often everyday language does not help, for children may not realise that we are speaking metaphorically when we talk about 'a living flame', 'feeding plants'. etc.

There has been extensive research into primary children's ideas about things in the world around them, often revealed through their drawings, actions and writing as well as discussion (as we shall see later, in Chapter 7). One example of a misconception is provided by some children who were investigating changes in materials. They were looking at metal surfaces and at the rusting on some of them. They had some nails which were shiny as well as ones which were rusty, and they were observed to be scraping the surface of the shiny nails. When asked about what they were doing they said they wanted 'to find the rust underneath'. Although this may seem strange, it only takes a moment to realise that children regularly observe rust beneath flaking paint on cars, bicycles and railings. So why not under the surface of the nail? Indeed the 'unscientific' ideas that children reveal are generally found to have some basis in their experience and are not just the product of childish fantasy. Characteristically their immature ideas arise from:

- paying attention to one feature as a cause of a particular effect and ignoring the possibility of a combination of factors (as in considering all that plants need to grow is water);

- depending on what they perceive rather than the logic which may suggest a different interpretation (as in the case of the 'magnetic' wooden blocks – see below);

- picking up words without grasping their full meaning (e.g. recognising that sound travels in some materials as vibrations but not realising that sound *is* vibration);

- not testing out ideas to see if there is evidence to support them, or testing them in an unsystematic way;

- having insufficient evidence against which to test their ideas because of their limited experience and so thinking that the ideas apply generally when in fact they don't (e.g. 'all wood floats – unless you have tried ebony!');

- lack of access to alternative ideas that would fit the evidence better – in such circumstances all learners hold onto existing ideas rather than have no idea at all.

These features of children's thinking are all good reasons for taking children's ideas seriously, which means recognising that they exist, that there is some reason for them and that they should be the starting point for change towards more scientific ideas. The characteristics also give some clues as to how to go about this, for example, by providing more experiences for testing the ideas, by extending the range of ideas that they have access to, by discussing the meaning they understand for certain words they use, by helping them to develop the process skills which will help them to test their ideas more rigorously. We pick up these points again in Chapter 7.

Children's process skills

These, too, can be limited and 'everyday' rather than systematic. Take, for instance, some children who noticed that blocks of smooth, varnished wood stuck together when wet, and immediately described the wood as 'magnetic' (see Harlen, 1993). They were ignoring some available evidence in doing this (e.g. there were ways in which the blocks did not behave as magnets – there was no repulsion, only the sticking together, and for this the blocks had to be wet). They might have dismissed the idea if they had systematically considered the common features of magnets they had seen before and the wood blocks. It was the process of linking the scientific idea of magnetism (very useful in understanding other experiences, but not this one) to the experience, not the idea itself, which was at fault in this case.

So, it is not difficult to imagine that an inappropriate idea could be accepted, or an appropriate idea rejected when it should not be, depending on how the checking is done.

For example, in the fabrics activity in Chapter 2, children will probably have used ideas from their different past experiences to suggest which was the best fabric for 'keeping us dry':

'This one, because it's thickest' (the thicker the better).

'This one, because it's like my raincoat' (and mine keeps me dry).

'This one, because it's that sort of stuff that most raincoats are made out of' (so it must be best).

Now suppose the children tested the fabrics by comparing the thickness only. They would gain little information which would help them in answering the question posed, for they would have made a comparison which was not relevant to it.

More generally, this is a common error of processing, where there is failure to identify the relevant variable to measure or compare. An everyday example is deciding which article to buy on the basis of the 'free offer' that comes with it, rather than on which is really more suitable for our purposes.

Another type of error in processing would occur if the children were testing the fabrics with water but did this by pouring different amounts on to the fabrics so that fair comparison was not possible. The answer would also be unhelpful in answering the problem.

Whilst in these cases it may not matter if the children decide that fabric B rather than fabric C is the 'best', it isn't difficult to think of instances where the consequences can have a longer-term effect on children's ideas. Imagine children setting up two simple electric circuits:

- one with red wires and a low-powered battery;

- one with blue wires and a higher-powered battery.

By comparing the brightness of the bulbs, it would be possible to conclude that the blue wires made the bulb brighter, unless the children realised that they were not making a fair comparison.

Developing ideas and using process skills

Our reasons for emphasising the use of science process skills is not, then, just for their own sake. Yes, it is good for children to be able to test things and check ideas in a fair way, but just as important a reason is that this is the only way in which they will build up useful ideas or concepts.

We will say a little more about what these useful concepts are in Chapter 10. For the moment we focus on the *process of change* in children's ideas, a process in which children use and check their ideas. A few examples help to show how the level of the children's development of skills affects the development of their ideas.

1. *Take observation* for a start. Low-level development of this skill is characterised by global rather than detailed observation, attention to what is expected rather than what is actually there and a greater attention to differences than to similarities. Children whose observation is characterised in this way may easily miss the detail which enables them, for instance, to distinguish old bricks from new ones, to notice patterns in the way bricks are laid, to detect the signs of weathering on walls, or, in a different context, to notice that plants grow better in some conditions than in others – all observations which in themselves provide evidence allowing ideas to be checked.

2. *Predicting* is a skill which greatly affects the extent to which ideas are advanced by testing. Using ideas to make a prediction provides opportunities to test their application in other situations, and so change them into more widely usable ideas. It has a central part in helping the children to verify or modify their ideas.

When the skill is not well developed children's 'predictions' are close to 'guesses', not really arising from ideas based on evidence and therefore not taking a large part in the development of those ideas. A child whose prediction skills are more advanced will have a reason for suggesting, for instance, that things that dissolve in water might do so more quickly if warm water is used, and testing this prediction will be helping to check his or her idea. These are important reasons for helping children from the 'guessing' stage to more advanced stages in the skill of prediction.

3. *Using fair testing* in investigations provides another clear example of how processes influence what is learned from an activity. When objects or materials are compared one with another then not only are the materials being tested but there is an idea being checked, e.g. that adding salt to tap water will stop soap dissolving in it (after observing the difficulty of making a lather in sea-water), or that this kind of wood is more 'bendy' than that kind.

Young children or those at an immature level in fair-testing skills may not keep the amount of water and of soap the same in making the test of the effect of salt; they may compare a thick piece of one kind of wood with a thin piece of the other; they may, indeed, make a comparison which does not relate to the problem at all, perhaps using the appearance or hardness of the wood as a basis for judgement. What happens to their ideas about the effect of salt in water or the properties of wood is not difficult to imagine.

The role of process skills and attitudes

What we want is for children to obtain evidence which helps them to change their initial, limited ideas into more widely applicable and helpful ones (see Chapter 10). We can see that this change depends on how they obtain the evidence, as well as on what their ideas are and the nature of the problem.

The role of process skills in the development of children's ideas in science is the reason why it is necessary to emphasise skills in science activities and to foster attitudes which control their use. The attitudes include:

- curiosity (willingness to question, eagerness to explore);

- respect for evidence (willingness to collect and use evidence);

- flexibility (willingness to change ideas in the face of evidence);

- critical reflection (the habit of reflecting on and critically reviewing ways in which an investigation has been carried out).

Learning with understanding

The view that learning involves changing ideas also helps to explain why it isn't enough to tell children how things work or provide information from books. This is because:

- facts which don't link into existing ideas don't affect the way children really understand the world around, any more than learning rhymes and jingles by heart;

- children still use their own ideas in explaining things to themselves, even though they may be able to recite the 'right' answers they have been given.

To bring change in the children's own ideas, we have to help them to change these ideas for themselves by realising that they do not fit evidence, or not as well as alternative ideas do. We cannot do the changing for them. All we can do is to help them in the process by providing opportunities for ideas to be tried out, challenged, extended, changed or replaced.

We must not forget, of course, that we are concerned with young children, whose experience and ways of thinking are limited. This means that if we rely too much on their narrow range of existing ideas they may not be able to understand new experience; it is important for them to realise that there are other ideas besides their own to be tried. This is where discussion is so important, for it exposes children to what others think and to a range of suggestions to try out beyond the ones they themselves have thought of.

When children begin to realise the advantages of considering alternative ideas, they should be able to look for these in books and other sources of information. These sources should not be offered as giving the 'right' answers, but rather as providing suggestions that are worthwhile considering.

So we need to provide the materials, the talk, the right kinds of questions and, above all, the supportive atmosphere in which children can expose and change their ideas without being made to feel they were 'wrong'. Bringing all this together, we can now use the decision-making framework described on page 22 to summarise the experiences, organisation, roles and evaluation criteria for this kind of learning.

1. View of learning

Children learn with understanding by:

- making their own sense of experience;
- linking new experience to existing ideas and past experience;
- changing ideas to fit evidence better.

2. Learning experiences

Experiences which provide opportunities for learning of this kind are those in which children:

- actively seek evidence through the senses;
- check ideas against evidence;
- take account of others' ideas;
- seek more effective ways of testing ideas.

3. Materials, the roles of teacher and pupils in interacting with them, and the necessary organisation

The role of materials is:

- to arouse curiosity and stimulate exploration and investigation;
- to provide evidence and means of testing predictions.

The role of the teacher is:

- to find out children's existing ideas and help children to test predictions based on them;
- to help children devise and reflect upon ways of testing predictions fairly;

- to promote interaction with materials and others' ideas.

The role of the children is:

- to become involved in raising questions, discussing ideas and in making predictions and proposing ways of testing them.

The organisation should be such as to:

- optimise opportunity to interact with real materials;
- optimise access to a range of ideas from other children, adults, books and other media.

4. Evaluation criteria

The criterion for learning opportunities is:

- the extent to which the children have the experiences indicated in the checklists on page 12 of Chapter 3.

The criterion for children's learning is:

- their progress in developing skills, attitudes and concepts as identified here and assessed by the methods discussed in Chapters 7 and 8.

Where is this way of working leading us?

Hopefully it is now possible to see the purposes of the kinds of experiences we are suggesting. The summary in Table 4.1 brings together the reasons in terms of children's learning for the suggestions made about organising classroom work.

What to do	Where it leads
Provide materials and arrange for children to interact with them and with other real things in the environment	Children gather evidence using their own senses and through their own activity; check their ideas against this evidence of how real things behave
Organise activities to encourage discussion in small groups	Children hear ideas other than their own, refine their own through explaining them and have a range of suggestions to try
Discuss with children in small groups or individually	Children talk about their ideas so that these are evident to themselves and the teacher; they are encouraged to check their findings, to think critically about what they have done and how they have done it; teachers offer ideas and direct children to sources of information if relevant
Hold whole-class discussion and reporting sessions	Children record/report for a purpose; listen to and discuss what others have done; realise that there are different approaches (and results) from theirs
Make available books, displays and pictures in the classroom and give access to sources of information outside	Children compare their ideas with others'; gain information to extend or change their ideas, possibly to raise questions leading to further enquiries
Teach the conventions used in graphs, tables, charts, etc. and the techniques of using measuring instruments	Children are able to use quantitative techniques when they wish to; they can increase the accuracy of measurement; they can choose appropriate forms of communication

Table 4.1 Rationale for the approach

5
PLANNING AND DEVELOPING ACTIVITIES

In Chapter 2 we described, in some detail, one sequence for developing investigational work and in Chapter 3 we analysed the experience. But there is a considerable gulf between following this sequence and having the confidence to organise science using a similar approach as a regular part of practice.

In this and the next chapter we acknowledge the real concerns about planning and organising science for a whole class within a whole curriculum, for a whole year, and offer practical suggestions for approaching the task.

Planning science work

General guidelines on skills and content to be taught are to be found in national or local curriculum documents, providing a framework within which to plan at the school and class level; but they do not spell out the activities nor the organisation as we did in Chapter 2. This level of detailed planning is best done by the class teacher.

The point is that if we genuinely want children to learn with understanding and to develop their own ideas, it is bound to be necessary to adapt or create activities suited to their particular starting points. Available classroom materials provide ideas for activities and organisation, but the teacher will have to decide what is best for his or her class at a particular time. Thus the principles of planning, developing and organising science work will always be important to the teacher. The following questions are bound to come to mind in relation to these matters:

- How does planning at the national, school and class levels fit together?

- How do I get ideas for developing children's investigative science work?

- How do I fit science into the rest of the curriculum?

- How do I organise the children so that they can gain most benefit from investigative work and from discussion?

- How do I cope with obtaining and organising materials and equipment?

Here we will deal with the first two of these questions; the others will be taken up in Chapter 6.

Planning within local or national guidelines

Three levels of planning are indicated in the Table 5.1, together with the main functions of the planning at each level.

Planning at the school level is important so that all teachers feel that their work is fitting into the progressive learning of their children. It is increasingly common for this to be done by the whole staff planning together and usually focuses on deciding how the national or local curriculum will be 'translated' into a school programme. For example, one junior school working through science-based topics agreed a programme of five topics per year (one each half of the term – or about six weeks – except the summer term) as given in Table 5.2.

This programme was given a great deal of thought and school-based planning in terms of the resources needed, and it would have to stay in place for some years. This is fine as long as the

Level of planning	Main functions of planning at this level
National, state or local	• To ensure a common entitlement for all children • To provide for continuity in progression through schooling (and particularly from primary to secondary school) • To guide school-level planning so that aims and objectives are 'in the right ball park'
School (institution)	• To ensure continuity of progression within the school • To identify content areas and contexts (topics) suited to the school environment • To avoid repetition, gaps and unplanned overlap between one class and another
Class	• To decide the particular aspects of topics to be the focus of investigations • To ensure that appropriate skills, ideas and attitudes will be developed through the topic • To prepare the class organisation, materials and equipment likely to be needed • To consider assessment and teaching methods suited to the subject matter

Table 5.1 Levels of curriculum planning

Year 3	Year 4	Year 5	Year 6
Homes The weather Sound and music Plants and growth Making circuits	Ourselves Communications Reflections Journey into space Water	Materials Growing Electricity Buildings and structures Toys and games	The surface of the Earth Light and shadows On the move Earth in space Keeping healthy

Table 5.2 A junior school programme of science-based topics

topics do not become 'stale' by repetition year after year. This can easily be avoided, however, using some of the ideas we suggest in the next section, for these will ensure that the topic work – on buildings, in this case – can never be repeated in exactly the same way.

Planning at the school level is mainly concerned with the knowledge and understanding that can be developed through particular content. The skills and attitudes are relevant – and should be applied – in all activities so don't appear in relation to planning content or topics, except as a list constantly to be kept in mind.

However careful and well constructed the planning at the school or local level, it cannot encompass the detailed planning that individual teachers must do. It is at the class level of planning where the skills have to be matched in detail to the subject matter. Agreed topics can be taught in a variety of ways, as

we saw at the beginning of Chapter 4. So how can teachers go about developing the work so that children are involved in investigation and are developing their ideas through practical testing? How do they decide, for example:

• how children are to interact with the materials?

• what skills are to be used?

• what 'small' ideas will be developed which relate to the 'big' ideas specified in the school plan?

These are the matters to which we now turn.

Getting ideas for children's activities

This aspect of planning consists of looking at possibilities in the chosen topic or content area and then working out how to convert these into action in the classroom. Thus the two steps we will discuss are:

- identifying the 'science potential' in everyday things and situations;

- converting this potential into 'action questions' that can shape children's investigations.

Seeing the potential

Let's take as an example possibilities for work on *buildings*. Much general potential for science can be identified if we scan the topic in terms of its opportunities for skills development (a skills scan), bearing in mind that these skills relate to obtaining and organising evidence and require the children to have direct contact with materials.

Hence the first planning decision is a fairly obvious one, namely what can the children investigate? Possibilities are:

- building materials;

- actual buildings;

- building-site activities.

Given all or some of these resources, a skills scan involves asking a number of questions to identify general possibilities. Table 5.3 provides an example of what might emerge.

Notice that:

- for scanning purposes a short list of skills has been used. This is useful for first-stage planning; other opportunities relating to the full list of skills can be accommodated at a later stage;

- the possibilities are speculative. This is because they are not yet shaped sufficiently to indicate particular investigations children could undertake. For this to happen they need 'converting' to specific challenges.

Producing 'action questions' from general possibilities

The ability to convert general possibilities into 'action questions' for children to tackle is probably the most important skill in planning science work. Like other skills it develops well with practice and it becomes a comparatively easy task if approached systematically.

We will develop the approach by considering particular possibilities for investigating a school building, since this is a resource available to every teacher. Systematic thinking to identify action questions will run along these lines:

'If X is what children encounter and Y is the general skill possibility I have in mind, then

Skills-scanning questions	General possibilities
What might they observe?	Detail and pattern in particular building materials or in buildings and in their parts? Comparisons between different materials and different building constructions?
What might they predict?	Changes in building materials? How long will a change, e.g. concrete setting, take?
What might they investigate (test)?	Properties of building materials? of building tools? and machines?
What might they design and make?	Build a simulated house? Make machines for lifting, carrying?

Table 5.3 General possibilities derived by skills-scanning

what questions will initiate activities so that the children:
– have a problem to investigate?
– can tackle the problem in ways that foster development of that skill?'

Let's see how the approach can work out in practice.

Possibilities for observation

If X is the school building and Y the observation possibilities from Table 5.3, namely noticing detail and pattern and making comparisons, then action questions abound:

● How many different kinds of materials can you see? (Note that this question is preferable to one that asks children to name the materials present.)

● Which materials can you see in many places? Which in only a few? Are any found in one place only?

● How many different shapes can you see? Which is the commonest shape? Which is the least common?

● How many different parts of the building can you identify?

● Which parts are solid? Which hollow?

● Which parts let things through? Which keep things out?

● Which parts join things? Which separate things?

● Are all similar parts exactly the same? Do different parts have things in common?

Of course X could be part of a building, say a wall, rather than the entire structure, and in this case action questions that encourage observation include:

● Are all bricks (stones) in the wall exactly the same?

● How many differences are there between two bricks of the same kind? How many similarities?

● How many bricks does one brick touch?

● How many different things are there on the wall/in the wall?

● Is there any pattern in their distribution?

The emphasis is on producing questions that will get children looking closely so that they see things not noticed before and experience things which help them to build up *ideas* of similarity and difference, of relationships between whole things and their parts, and of causal rather than chance distribution in person-made structures.

None of the questions identified requires of teachers in-depth scientific knowledge and most are of the kind that would be asked by any teacher wishing to engage children in first-hand observation. Indeed it is difficult to claim that these questions are particularly scientific – they could equally well lead to activities in other areas of the curriculum. But their relevance across the curriculum does not diminish their value as precursors to activities of a scientific nature.

Activities involving predicting and fair testing are at the heart of the science curriculum – and, because technology is closely related to a subject such as building, we have included some possibilities for designing and making in Table 5.3 too. These science/technology activities tend to be lacking in many children's experience because teachers are uncertain of how they can be developed. The approach we are adopting can, by starting from observation, stimulate many other possibilities for scientific activity.

Possibilities for predicting

'Predicting' activities are ones that involve children going beyond their present experiences and observations in some way. They must be firmly rooted in these experiences and must enable children to use and test out ideas they have about what they have seen or done. They take the children from exploring *what is* to exploring *what might be*. For example:

● Would a wall twice as thick be twice as strong? (Based on the idea, supported by observation, that thicker walls are stronger, and leading to a prediction that a wall twice as thick would be twice as strong.)

- Will the mortar set more quickly if we use warm water?
  (Based on everyday experience, e.g. in cooking, that heat often speeds up changes and leading to a prediction to be tested that warm water will shorten the setting time.)

- Will it be easier to lift the bucket if we use a larger cotton reel for a pulley?
  (Based on an idea about how the pulley helps and leading to a prediction to be tested that the larger the pulley the more it helps.)

It doesn't matter that some predictions will be disproved (as in two of the examples given above); in fact it is most important to encourage children to test out all their predictions. As we discussed in Chapter 4, this is essential to the development of their ideas. It is necessary, however, to help them distinguish between a guess, for which they have no basis in experience, and a prediction, which is using their experience.

So, when children make a prediction, or ask a question which implies a prediction, it is a good idea to ask them 'Now why do you think that might happen?' or 'What makes you want to try that?' By doing so not only will you learn a lot about their thinking, but it will help the children to sort out their ideas to try to explain them. But don't make it an inquisition. If the children can't explain, then let them carry straight on to test their idea in practice.

As the examples in Table 5.3 show, some prediction activities may have a time dimension. With this in mind, action questions related to, say, observing walls, would be of the kind:

- Which things are there all the time?

- Which are there some of the time?

- Will it look exactly the same tomorrow/next week/next term?

Children will need to think about the questions, perhaps recording what they expect to happen, and later check their ideas against actual events.

Possibilities for investigating (testing)

Table 5.3 notes as general possibilities under this heading testing the 'properties of building materials'. There is tremendous potential here, but how to convert it into action questions? We need a framework for thinking, for example along the following lines.

1. *What are the significant properties/features of the materials?* One significant property of a wall is that it is strong. Children will be aware of this, at least implicitly. They can be encouraged to observe different patterns used in the construction of walls. Suitable action questions would then be:

- Which pattern is strongest?

- Is this pattern stronger than that?

2. *What situations will encourage children's awareness of these properties/features so that they can appreciate variables and attempt to control them?* A significant feature of most walls is that the bricks or stones are joined together by something (mortar). Children can observe this directly. They can be encouraged to find ways of joining bricks/stones using mortar. Some action questions would be:

- Which method makes the strongest join?

- Which mix sets first?

3. *What forms of question will focus their work towards handling variables?* By applying the approach with X as the school building and Y as investigating (testing), a variety of action questions emerge. They can be grouped into possible general forms:
(a) Which ... is best for ... ? e.g.

- Which method is best for protecting woodwork?

- Which product is best for cleaning windows?

- Which mix makes the strongest concrete?

(b) Is it true that ... ? e.g.

- reinforced concrete is stronger than non-reinforced concrete?

- smoke rises further from tall chimneys than from short ones?

(c) Which ... is/does ... ? e.g.

- Which door is easiest to open?

- Which window lets in most light?

- Which kind of brick absorbs most water?

- Which concrete mix sets faster?

With practice, questions such as these form quickly, whatever the nature of X.

Possibilities for designing and making

Let's turn now to 'design-and-make' work. General possibilities, as recorded in Table 5.3, emerge by considering the particular constructions and 'things that work' associated with a topic, but further thinking is needed to convert these into action questions.

1. *What experience will children need to appreciate the structure/function of the real thing?* For children to appreciate the construction of a building they need to have observed its component parts and to have some appreciation of the sequence of events in its development. This latter can be achieved ideally through watching building-site activities; more conveniently by learning about events from information books.

2. *What might they do/use to simulate its structure/ function?* The sequence

building plot → foundation → walls, doors, window spaces → roof

could be simulated on a small scale, say a seed-tray-sized plot. Children could make concrete foundations for walls, use lolly sticks for roof trusses and hang tiles made from thin plastic.

3. *What are the key questions that will make their work purposeful and not just making for making's sake?* Such questions might be:

- What shall we use for making .... ? (teacher's ideas are long-stop possibilities)

- How can we make sure that ... ? (as in the real thing), e.g.
  - a wall is vertical?
  - a roof has the required slope?
  - the concrete has the required consistency?

Such questions are appropriate also for simulating things that work. For instance, a machine that will lift a bucket from floor to roof height which, in a simple form, could be made from a cotton reel, string, and a yoghurt pot. Its making might be stimulated by seeing the real thing in action or an illustration in a book. For this, as with all 'working things' children make, a further key question is:

- How could we make it work better? e.g.
  - lift more quickly?
  - lift more steadily?
  - lift with less effort?

Again, such questions will come readily with practice.

Further possibilities for making working things relating to buildings include:

- a spirit level;

- scaffolding;

- a crane;

- a concrete mixer.

These kinds of activity need more scientific knowledge on the part of the teacher and more resources than observational activities. But experience shows that, almost inevitably, the necessary ideas and most of the resources will come from the children, if their teacher is willing to 'have a go'.

Putting ideas into practice

It should be apparent from the preceding analyses that there is no shortage of ideas for science activities if they are sought systematically. Indeed teachers who regularly use the approach described above find this aspect of planning fairly easy; their major task becomes one of selecting, from the wide range of possibilities, a suitable starting point and anticipating its likely development so that the work overall has a reasonable skills coverage.

Figure 5.1 shows one teacher's forecast for developing a topic on walls with 5–6 year olds. Figure 5.2 is a record showing the sequence of events that actually took place.

A few significant points to notice in Figs. 5.1 and 5.2 are:

● the use of action questions in the forecast to indicate possibilities;

● the way in which possible activities are linked in the forecast but not rigidly sequenced;

● that although both forecast and record have the same starting point, the actual development was sequenced to respond to children's particular interests as the work progressed.

Going further

This planning approach can be used in a wide range of topics; it can be adapted, for instance, to apply to the general topic *food*.

1. Identify its general possibilities (as in Table 5.3).
2. Convert these possibilities to action questions.
3. Construct a forecast scheme of work for a class.

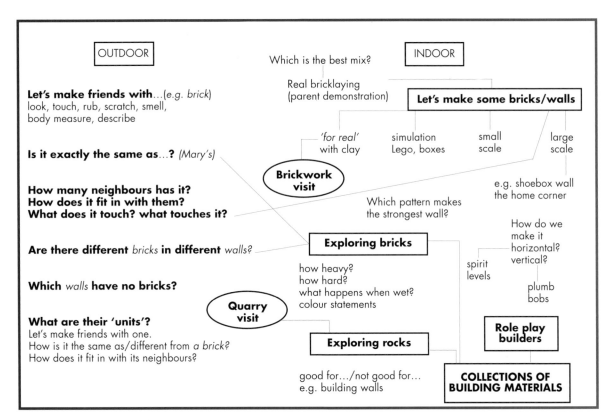

Fig.5.1 Exploring walls: forecast

Starting point:
Making friends with a brick in the school wall
    Rubbings; counting its neighbours
    Observing detail
    Comparing with a stone in another wall
    Finding 'different kinds of' walls
    Collecting observations of things in and on walls
    Comparing own brick with another 'kind of' brick

A brick collection
    Sorting and ordering
    Comparing 'ordinary' and sea-worn bricks of the same kind (locating the manufacturer's name on the bricks)
    Collecting 'what will happen if . . . ' questions
    Collecting 'I wonder why . . . ' questions

Making model walls
    Free building with big Lego
    Task building of different bonding patterns
    Making spirit levels and plumb lines to check horizontal and vertical
    Which pattern makes the strongest wall?
    Inventing a 'wall-basher'; discussing fairness of test and modifying

Making concrete bricks
    Examining ready-mix concrete; separating and describing parts
    'Guestimating' how many measures to fill the mould
    Exploring mixing to produce a 'nearly solid' mix
    Predicting when the concrete will set

Making a brick wall
    Examining own-made bricks; noticing differences
    Discussing reasons; comparing own brick with teacher-made bricks
    Examining ready-mix mortar; noticing differences in sand and cement components; relating to ready-mix concrete
    Mixing mortar; using simulated trowels to lay home-made bricks in a stretcher-bond pattern

Relating walls to other parts of a building
    'Making friends' with doors, windows, floors, roofs
    Collecting observations of similarity and difference in each
    Collecting ideas for experiments concerning functions of parts
    Sequencing events in building construction via picture cards
    House building on a seed-box-sized 'plot'; plans
    'Digging' and laying concrete foundations; wall building

Relating bricks to other building materials
    Exploring a collecting of building materials
    Grouping and sequencing concerning use, properties and location
    Collecting 'let's find out . . . ' questions
    Junk modelling of a building to simulate real locations and functions

Sharing experience and broadening concept of walls
    Class forum with questions to panel of 'experts' on walls of buildings and building materials
    Collecting and discussing ideas for further investigations of walls via picture situation cards

Fig. 5.2 Exploring walls: record of work

6

CURRICULUM AND CLASSROOM ORGANISATIONS

The planning approach suggested in the previous chapter should help teachers find ideas for children's activities. But however exciting the possibilities for particular activities the work will not be developed strongly unless we consider the problems of:

- how to fit science into the rest of the curriculum?

- how to organise the children so that they can gain most benefit from investigative work and from discussion?

- what to do about resources and organising materials to ensure the work runs smoothly?

These matters are considered in this chapter. Some aspects of the first and third of these depend upon decisions made at the school level, but all are ones with which the individual teacher has ultimately to be concerned. Moreover, they all involve choices which each have advantages and disadvantages. In weighing these up we should again remind ourselves that the organisation has to be chosen to support the kind of learning that we want to bring about in children, and the approach to teaching which we have suggested is suited to providing for this.

Curriculum organisation

In general, primary teachers have three main ways of giving curriculum time to science:

(a) reserving a regular, fixed time for science lessons;
(b) using less frequent but longer periods of time for science-based topics;
(c) integrating science with other curriculum areas in topic work.

Two issues are intertwined here: the extent to which science is integrated with other areas of the curriculum and the way time for science is organised.

Pros and cons of broad-based topics

Take the first of these issues relating to curriculum organisation: the extent to which science is seen as being part, along with other subject areas, of broad topics. Advantages that have been claimed for fully integrated topic work include those summarised in Table 6.1; against these are the disadvantages that experience of cross-curricular topic work has thrown up. Except in the hands of the most gifted teacher, who can identify and develop learning in science within any topic (and do this for all the other subject areas, too), this organisation has significant disadvantages from the point of view of children's science activities.

Most of the advantages in Table 6.1 can in fact be gained through topics that are science-based. Children can be working on different aspects and so be developing their own ideas, and not needing the same resources at the same time. Yet the common topic will ensure that there is relevance and interest in sharing ideas through the essential discussion of progress and findings.

There is always room for variation, of course, and some teachers of 8–12 year olds have found that merging two subjects can achieve greater time flexibility and is a powerful strategy for developing the work. Table 6.2 records some examples of subject mergers that have been used by teachers, developing from a separate-subject approach. Initially each merger was introduced purely as an organisational device to provide 'flexitime' for experimenting with new ways of working. Subsequently, the experience

Advantages	Disadvantages
• Creates opportunities for children to study parts of their environment without the artificiality of subject boundaries • Provides more flexible time for children to follow their own interests and design their investigations • Eases problems of shortage of equipment on account of the variety of activities on-going at any one time • It is more 'in tune' with the way children naturally learn	• The science component is fragmentary and often trivial • Continuity in development of ideas and skills is made more difficult • Topics range too widely and science is rarely treated in sufficient depth • Quite often the science disappears altogether, especially if the teacher lacks confidence in this area • Children, and in some cases, teachers, do not begin to identify what makes science a distinct area of study

Table 6.1 Advantages and disadvantages of fully integrated topic work

Subjects merged	Integrating topic	Examples of science component	Other subject focus
Science and maths	Ourselves	Who sees best? Is it true that big hands are stronger than small hands?	Graph work
Science and geography	Street study	Which shop sign is easiest to see? Shall we make a working model of a traffic light?	Mapping skills
Science and history	The Victorians	What was washday like without modern materials? – do detergents make washing easier? – which is the best place to dry wet clothes?	Understanding the lives of people of the past
Science and art and craft	Camouflage	How will the colour change if we ...? Is it true that background colour and pattern affect the way we see things?	Colour statements
Science and PE	Playground games	Which ball is the best bouncer? On which surface is it easiest to skip?	Small games skills

Table 6.2 Some examples of subject integration

gained led to mergers with other subject areas and the increased curriculum integration provided even greater time flexibility.

Organisation of time for science

The main difference between science-based topics and science lessons is the organisation of the time for science, the second issue mentioned in relation to curriculum organisation.

Teachers organising science as separate lessons will be devoting a regular amount of time to science but in short and limited periods. The disadvantages can be seen if we apply the Chapter 3 checklists (page 12) to the situation. A number of 'no' answers present themselves because of the difficulty of developing investigative problem-solving science in short, fixed periods of time. Children need ample time to discuss ideas, time to put these ideas into practical action whilst they are fresh in their minds and time also to make 'mistakes' and modify their work accordingly. This cannot be achieved in short lessons. Whilst not implying that science lessons are completely inappropriate, it is suggested that some rejigging of the class timetable may be needed if present practice is to put science in slots of half an hour or even an hour in duration.

Teachers facing the problem of a restrictive timetable have produced differing solutions. One teacher of 5–7 year olds, having gained some experience of investigative work, decided that a science day would be more appropriate than her timetabled weekly $1\frac{1}{2}$ hours. Two years on she still operates a science day and supports it, against challenges that it means less time for basic skill work, on the grounds that the day involves much maths activity and an enormous amount of language development.

A balanced approach

We can see that each of the three main patterns of curriculum organisation has advantages and disadvantages, which are summarised in Table 6.3. Our concern is not to establish which pattern is best, but to make clear the various pros and cons as a basis for decision-making. The aim over the long-term is a flexible organisation which accommodates them all at appropriate points. We do not want to debate here the quantity of time that science should receive; the question of the amount of science time

is not so much the issue (about 10% is now accepted as a reasonable aim) as the quality of what goes on in whatever time is available.

Classroom organisation: the children

There is no one organisation of the children that fits all science activities. Rather there is a place for children working

- as a whole class,
- in groups,
- in pairs,
- individually,

according to the nature of the work and subject to other considerations such as availability of resources. The kinds of work where each of these may be appropriate are summarised in Table 6.4. As can be seen, there is likely to be a case for more than one organisation within activities on a particular topic.

When groups are formed, or children work in pairs or individually, there is automatically, from any one child's point of view, less attention from

Science in the curriculum	Main advantage	Disadvantages
Separate lessons	Subject receives regular attention	Time restrictions can inhibit investigative work. Fixed time-slot can stifle spontaneity
As science-based topics	Coverage of content and progress in skills and ideas more easily planned	Links to other subjects may be lost unless specifically planned
As part of wider topics	Children's learning can be enriched and made more meaningful through links with other subject activities	Science can 'get lost' in a general topic and work is sometimes superficial. Links with other subjects can be spurious

Table 6.3 Advantages and disadvantages of different curriculum organisations

Class organisation	Where most appropriate
Whole class	• Teacher introducing a topic; giving a motivating demonstration; giving information about available materials, resources and points of safety; showing a technique that may be useful (how to make a rubbing, use a hand lens or a pooter to collect small insects, etc.) • Children sharing ideas and experiences
Group work (ideally groups of 4, but 5 or 6 for older children if neccesary)	• Exploration and investigation where genuine collaborative tasks can be set (each child has a role in the combined effort and all are aware of this) • Brainstorming about how events might be explained (hypothesising), or what results might mean • Discussion of ideas and findings with teacher • Teacher suggesting further experiences or ideas to try
Pairs	• Planning and carrying out investigations where close observation is needed and collaborative larger group work is not feasible • As for group work where number of roles within the task is limited
Individual	• Children expressing their own ideas; recording their work; finding information from books; practising new technique; gathering evidence to pool later in group or whole class.

Table 6.4 Ways of grouping children for science work

the teacher than in the whole-class situation. The trade-off for the child is more contact with materials and with their peers. It is important to keep a balance between these influences on the children. Materials and discussion with others are essential to learning, as we have stressed in Chapter 2, but left too much to themselves children's work can turn into 'blind alleys' and the teacher needs to be watchful to prevent this.

With group work the questions of size and composition of the groups arise. Although an optimum group size of four is indicated in Table 6.4, there always has to be a compromise determined by the size of the class and of the classroom. An important factor to keep in mind in relation to group size is the potential for genuine group working. Group work means a combined effort, not a collection of individuals working alone. Arranging this becomes more difficult the larger the group, but for all groups it is important for the group work to be set up so that members have a well-defined role and for the teacher to ensure that each member has the chance to take a full part.

The other question concerns how the children are to be formed into groups – by the teacher or by the children? Should groups be based on ability or experience, or should these be disregarded? Practice varies considerably in this matter. Often children continue to work in the same groups as are used for other subjects and so may implicitly be working in mathematics ability groups or in reading groups. Fortunately, achievement in science does not necessarily coincide with achievement in these other subjects, so the children may end up in mixed groups as far as science is concerned. We say 'fortunately' since research has shown that children's ideas progress to a greater degree when they work in heterogeneous groups than in homogeneous groups (Howe, 1990). There is a strong evidence that having *different* ideas expressed in the group enables all the children, of all abilities, to advance more than if they share much the *same* ideas. Moreover, the research showed that the effect was a lasting one, suggesting that exposure to ideas different from their own was an important factor in the development of each child.

Classroom organisation: materials and equipment

Obtaining and organising materials and equipment are major areas of demand in science and it is as well to acknowledge the fact. There are no universal procedures for instant success, but there is plenty of evidence that the tasks get easier with experience.

The two basic resourcing questions are:

- what materials and equipment are essential and how do I select and get what I need without excessive cost and effort?

- how do I organise and store the materials so that they are accessible for effective learning?

We will consider resourcing in terms of realistic provision and effective storage. We will not consider in detail all resources that ideally could support science. Curriculum programmes and teachers' guides generally contain comprehensive lists of what is required for particular activities (e.g. Nuffield Primary Science *Teacher's Guides*).

Realistic provision

It's useful to think of the materials children will need in three broad categories:

- everyday materials likely to be used whatever the topic for investigation;

- special equipment likely to be required for most topics;

- topic-related materials.

Everyday materials

These will be needed for activities involving making comparisons and for fair-testing. A useful starter list is:

- boxes, tins, bottles, tubs in a variety of materials and sizes;

- string, cotton, thread;

- paper clips, drawing pins, sticky tape;

- plasticine, straws, marbles, elastic bands;

- suitable adhesives.

Fortunately such materials are very easy to obtain and they will be accumulated as activities develop.

Special equipment

This will be needed to extend the children's own capabilities, helping them to observe more closely and enabling them to measure things. As a core collection, obtain:

- some means of magnifying;

- equipment for measuring time, length, mass, volume, temperature.

The exact nature of the equipment will depend on what is available in school. Most likely there will be maths equipment for basic measurement; magnifiers and thermometers are less common. If both of these are ideally needed but cannot be afforded, magnifiers will be the most useful investment.

Topic-related materials

These will be needed to stimulate the children's interests and ideas, and for particular investigations developed in the topic. This area of resourcing is likely to be the one that will need developing most strongly and we offer a well-tried common-sense strategy for approaching the task.

1. Decide on the topics that the class will investigate during the coming year.
2. For each topic:
   (a) list relevant things that children could examine to excite their interest. This will become the topic collection;
   (b) use a skills scan to get action questions for children's activities (see Chapter 5); anticipate and list the materials they will need to investigate them.
3. Assemble the materials! The exclamation mark is included because these three words mask the

considerable effort needed and it is at this point intentions can get lost in practical reality. For this reason it is helpful to enlist parent help. Many teachers have been amazed at the response to letters of the kind: 'We will soon be studying ... We need ... Can you help?' Experience shows that requests for specific items gain most response, though it is always worth adding 'and anything else you think might be useful'.

Planning along these lines will lead to a considerable increase in resources and so attention has to turn from 'How do I get them?' to 'How do I store them?'.

Effective storage

How and where science materials are stored will clearly depend on things such as money, space and the physical layout of a classroom. In deciding what will work best in the circumstances, it is useful to keep certain points in mind.

1. *It helps if the everyday materials needed for comparisons and fair testing are visually accessible to children.* Science activities have a strong inventive element, frequently involving the need to improvise. Being able to scan visually for possibilities helps children put their ideas into practical action, since they are not as adept as adults at 'seeing in the mind's eye'. Ways of achieving this include:

● using silhouettes of the contents on the outside of storage boxes;

● storing, as appropriate, in open-mesh or transparent containers;

● having a low-level 'you may need' table for small items;

● avoiding closed-cupboard storage.

It helps to use functional labels on storage containers. For example, 'length measurers' is more effective than 'rulers and tapes'; 'see-through things' communicates better than 'transparent objects'. This may seem a small point but it is quite important. Its effectiveness probably relates to the fact that investigative work requires children to become familiar with what

materials do and what they themselves can do to the materials. Cataloguing resources by descriptive name does not assist this process.

2. *It helps if topic-related materials are temporarily 'boxed' for easy distribution and retrieval.* In addition to collection boxes likely to be housed in a store cupboard, it is useful to consider boxing the materials that groups will need for investigative work over a period of a few weeks. The contents of these boxes will be determined by anticipating what children will need to respond to planned action questions. This arrangement will ease organisational problems, but it is not recommended as a long-term strategy for reasons identified below.

3. *It helps if children take responsibility for aspects of resourcing.* Responsibility for everyday materials can be given to 'storekeepers', whose job it is to keep things tidy and report when materials need replenishing. One infants teacher had fun labels for the children to identify particular responsibilities (for boxes, tubes, etc.).

More importantly, work will develop more purposefully when children take increased responsibility for the choice of materials they use. We will return to this point on page 45, but in the present context it means:

● making sure children are aware of the resources available to them, including those in the teacher's cupboard and in other parts of the school. Lists and simple catalogues will be needed and children can help in their compilation where feasible, older children could compile a database on a computer, of science equipment in the school;

● having 'house rules' that enable children to move freely and sensibly to get the materials they need.

These storage considerations are useful for shaping decisions, but there is one final point worth noting. As experience and confidence grow, storage arrangements are likely to change and some extension will be needed. Most commercial systems lack flexibility for coping with the variously sized objects that will accumulate and the need to classify for use. Unless a flexible ready-made system can be found, cardboard boxes, always the first aid to organisation, are likely to remain the best solution for many teachers.

Avoiding chaos

Science work is inevitably noisy work because we want children:

- to talk freely among themselves since this is necessary to shape their ideas;
- to work investigatively with materials.

In many investigations the materials themselves will increase the noise level, as when weights fall in a strength test. Additionally, some happenings will so engage the children that they will react excitedly. We cannot escape such working noise.

There will also be an element of mess because:

- everyday materials needed for investigation may well look untidy if stored accessibly and when in use as intended they may become an aesthetic eye sore;
- trial-and-error investigations will produce discarded items that temporarily add to the visual clutter and require attention in the clearing-up phase;
- liquids, however carefully handled, will sometimes get spilt.

These requirements understandably deter many teachers from developing genuinely investigative science. There is concern about accepting and coping with noise and mess and anxiety that things may get out of hand. Those worries are not groundless but, as is evident in classrooms where teachers are experienced in investigative work, commitment to the approach is not the same as commitment to chaos. How then to reduce its possibility?

It is necessary to accept that we cannot have a silent and immaculate classroom if we want to develop science work. Nevertheless, we do want noise and mess kept within reasonable bounds and there are strategies that are useful; some self-evident, some more subtle.

If the work is new to the children it helps if:

- early sessions do not involve too many dramatic happenings;
- resources can be obtained by the children with minimum fuss (see previous section);
- the number of children involved, at any one time, in practical testing activities is increased gradually, by initially staggering investigative work.

Less obviously – and crucially – it is important that we have clear ideas about how to ease children into new ways of working. When the children are not used to working with materials in an investigative manner and are then expected to do so they may be uncertain about the changed demands being made on them. Uncertainty causes confusion, and confusion can lead to unwanted off-task activity. This negative chain of events can be avoided if we help children make the transition, particularly in relation to their understanding of practical tasks and their use of materials.

In many situations the changed demands will be substantial, as indicated in Table 6.5.

Usual experience	New expectations
Told what to do	Expected to work things out for themselves
Given materials to work with	Expected to select appropriate materials themselves

Table 6.5 Changed demands on children

The change is too great for most children to cope with unaided; nor can many cope with it quickly. We can ease the transition by not expecting children to work unaided on very open problems until they have built up the appropriate experience.

Many problems, for example the question 'What ... is best for ...?' will initially be beyond most children's capabilities (unless they develop ideas through discussion with their teacher). Unaided groups will need to develop experience along the lines shown in Table 6.6.

Children's transition difficulties	Sequence of teacher help		
	1 ⟶	2 ⟶	3
Understanding what needs to be done	Do this ⟶ (full instructions given)	Try doing ⟶ (guidance with 'clues')	Invent a way to find out
Knowing which materials to use	Use these ⟶ (all necessary materials identified)	Use some or all of these ⟶ (some choice introduced)	Use what you need

Table 6.6 Supporting children's transition

The progression from 1 → 3 may take some children a term or more, but the sequence will help them to handle changed expectations and so will reduce the possibility of disorder.

Keeping going

Initially the development of active enquiry-based science is demanding, but the rewards are great. The following advice comes from teachers who have been through this stage and now organise investigative work as a matter of course:

● don't expect too much too soon;

● don't try to do too much too soon;

● have a phased plan for developing the work;

● give a high priority to children taking decisions about their work;

● make use of supportive resources such as TV programmes and work cards, but don't become dependent upon them;

● share your experience with colleagues.

That is sound advice and the thrust of this chapter has been directed towards helping the organisational decisions and practical action required for developing this type of work.

Finally, as preparation for further development, consider the activities identified in the 'Getting ideas' task of Chapter 5. How, in the light of this present chapter, could these be resourced and organised for classroom action?

7

USING ASSESSMENT TO HELP DEVELOPMENT OF IDEAS

The approach to learning that underpins this book aims at learning with understanding. As explained in Chapter 4, this means children making sense for themselves of the scientific aspects of the world around, a process in which they use existing ideas that come from previous experience. It is the teacher's role to help the children develop their ideas, but in order to do this he or she must know the starting point, that is, what are the ideas that children bring to their science work in school? Only then can the appropriate action be taken.

We have also pointed out that:

- the development of the children's ideas is dependent on the mental and physical skills the children use in processing information about objects, events and materials that they encounter;
- unless these skills develop from immature, 'everyday' forms to more mature and scientific forms then children are unlikely to develop scientific concepts with understanding (see pages 25 and 26).

Again, for the teacher to help this development he or she must know about the children's existing skills and attitudes as well their ideas. This calls for a particular kind of assessment that is integral to teaching and is the concern of this chapter and the next. We provide some ideas about how to find out where children are in development and, importantly, how to use this information in teaching, dealing first with children's ideas and then, in Chapter 8, with skills and attitudes.

Briefly, before that, since the word 'development' comes up so often in this discussion, it might be helpful to say something about its meaning to prevent possible misunderstanding.

The meaning(s) of development

In one sense 'development' implies an automatic process of change which will take place as a matter of course – the kind of 'development' which happens when a caterpillar changes into a butterfly. In another sense it implies a more active process, as when we talk of the 'development' of a programme of activities – by no means a spontaneous set of events! In both senses a series of changes is implied, but the supposed mechanism of the changes is different – internal in the case of the butterfly and external in the other case (programmes of activities do not develop themselves, unfortunately).

We are using the word here to mean the series of changes which take place in children's ideas, skills or attitudes. These changes are neither wholly spontaneous, taking place as a result only of maturation, nor wholly externally determined, taking place as a result of 'training'. The exact way in which the changes do take place is not known, but experience suggests that it is through a mixture of maturity and experience. There is evidence that, in science, children's ideas and skills could develop (i.e. pass through various changes) more quickly if children were given more opportunity for appropriate experience. But this isn't to say there is no limit set by mental maturity to the development.

In plain terms, what this means is:

- we shouldn't sit back and wait for ideas and skills to develop with time – that won't happen; on the other hand,
- we shouldn't expect to be able to accelerate children's progress through the developmental changes to an unlimited extent – change takes time.

One of the reasons for this latter point, as suggested in Chapter 4, is that these changes have to be brought about by the children themselves.

Although no-one can change the ideas or skills of another, it is the job of teachers to provide the conditions and encouragement for children themselves to make the changes which constitute development.

Ways of assessing children's ideas as part of teaching

Here is an activity that will reveal children's ideas about a particular event. It can be used as an exercise to try out various ways of gathering information about children's ideas, or introduced at a relevant point in children's activities, or just read through as a basis for applying the techniques in other areas of work.

The activity can be carried out with the whole class or with three or more groups, as convenient. The equipment needed is a collection of cleaned empty food cans, with labels removed so that the shiny metal surface is revealed, and some ice cubes (enough for about four cubes per can).

1. Arrange the children in groups of four, each group having two cans and some ice cubes. Then set tasks for the groups as follows:

   - *Group 1* – They are to put the ice in the bottom of the can and watch what happens. Then ask them, as a group, but without the teacher's help, to think of as many different explanations as they can of what they see happening on the outside of the can. Tell them to consider each explanation and to give each member of the group chance to say whether they agree with it or not, and why. Then they should prepare to tell the teacher about their ideas and reasons. Give the group about fifteen minutes for this task, but longer if the discussion is clearly still on-going after this time.

   - *Group 2* – Start this group in exactly the same way as group 1, but instead of preparing to talk about their ideas after their joint discussion, ask each one to write down the explanation(s), with reasons, which they think most likely.

   - *Group 3* – Ask this group to work in two pairs, each having one can and some ice. After they have put the ice in the can and watched what happens, ask each individually to draw a picture, or a series of pictures, that explains what they saw happening. Suggest that they put labels on their drawing and use words to help explain their ideas.

2. In all cases, in setting the task make sure that the words in which it is put express interest in the children's ideas, not whether or not they know the 'right' answer. So it is essential to phrase the request as 'What do you think is the explanation?' or 'Draw what *you* think is happening to cause what you see'.

3. If there are more than three groups, duplicate the groups with a particular tasks as required.

4. Whilst the children are working, the teacher should make sure that he or she is within listening distance of group 1 and should take note of how they are explaining things to each other and of the ideas they are considering. This listening in shouldn't be made obvious and direct interaction with the children should be avoided until the point where they are asked to report to the teacher on their ideas. This report is to the teacher in the group, not to the whole class. All the ideas that are offered should be accepted without comment at this stage.

5. Collect the writing and drawings from the other children, making sure that their meaning can be understood (if not, ask the child for an explanation and make a note on the work so that the intended meaning can be recalled later).

6. When all the ideas have been collected, in their various forms, there will be a range of ideas, some of which will no doubt be a surprise. Previous work on this subject has shown children often consider that the water on the outside of the can has leaked through from the melting ice inside, or that 'fumes' of cold have risen from the ice and

formed drops on the outside, or that it is their breath that has formed the mist. Whatever the ideas – and whether or not they are scientifically 'correct' – they can be the basis for investigation.

The next steps would be to work with the children to plan fair tests that would show which of all these ideas fits new evidence the best. What has been done can be regarded as the 'preliminary exploration' phase (see Chapter 2) and the next phase would be investigation. But we will not take this activity further at this point, because we want to reflect on what was being done in relation to assessing children's ideas.

Finding out children's ideas

In this exercise some of the most useful ways of gaining access to children's ideas have been used. Explicitly, these techniques involved:

- asking children to talk about their ideas to each other in a pupil-only discussion and *listening* to how they explain things or what they predict will happen;

- asking children to talk about their ideas to the teacher, after having opportunity to observe and form their ideas about possibilities;

- asking children to write about their ideas after a time for observation and reflection;

- asking children to draw their ideas, and annotate their drawings, either as a single drawing or a sequence of drawings.

The activity was designed to give experience of all of these techniques and probably some were rather more useful than others in this particular context. The purpose here was not to compare their effectiveness but to experience them in practice. In general one or two of these techniques would be used in a particular context, chosen to suit the nature of the content.

If it was not appropriate to use the shiny can as a basis for trying out these techniques, then instead, having read through what is involved, the techniques could readily be applied to other activities. For example:

- if children are about to study seeds and how they germinate, ask them to talk or write about or draw what they think is inside a seed, before they cut one open or try to make seeds grow;

- if they are about to embark on a study of sound, use the same techniques to find out what they think makes the sound when a guitar string is plucked and how they hear the sound;

- if the topic is the solar system, ask them to predict where they think the sun will be in the sky at a certain time in the day, after observing its position earlier, and to give their ideas to explain any change in position.

Using the information to help development of ideas

Next steps for the children

The suggestions just made have been expressed in terms of finding children's ideas at the start of a topic or series of activities. As such, it is important to use this information in deciding the next steps that the children need to take to advance their ideas towards the accepted scientific ones. Having done this, of course, the same kinds of techniques can be used to see if the children's ideas have in fact progressed.

The next steps for the children will depend on the particular ideas that they have. The steps will be in the direction of forming ideas that fit the evidence available and which become 'bigger' (more widely applicable) as the children gain more experience. We shall say more about the development towards 'big' ideas in Chapter 10. Here we are concerned with how to identify the next steps and this is best done through some examples.

In the ice-in-the-can activity, one group told the teacher about the ideas they had agreed:

'We saw that the wet stuff on the outside was just level with the ice on the inside and we think that what happens is that the cold from the ice sort of goes up in fumes into the air - you can't see it, but its like the currents in the air that you can't see - and then it comes down again on the outside. We think that eventually all the ice will melt and then this will stop.'

The teacher responded: 'That's an interesting idea. So what do you think will happen if you put a lid on the tin, just after putting the ice in it?' The children disagreed about whether this would stop the mist forming on the outside and decided to try it out.

When the teacher returned after they had found that the mist still formed, she helped them to another idea by asking them where they had seen 'mist' like this in other places. They found they could increase the moisture by breathing on the can. She asked them to try a can without ice in it and this led them to link the temperature of the can to the appearance of the mist. They then began to use this idea to explain the other examples of mist forming on surfaces that they had recalled.

In a different activity, about forces and movement, Amanda and her partner were dropping equal-sized pieces of paper, some crushed into balls and some left flat. Afterwards she wrote:

> When Colin dropped the 10×10 ball and the other 10×10 ball both hit the floor together. When I tried the 10×10 ball and the 10×10 sheet the ball hit the ground first because the gravity was round the ball and the air was under the sheet making it float.

Amanda is using the word 'gravity' without giving any indication that she understands it as a downward force with the air resistance being a force opposing the downwards movement. Discussion with Amanda about what she had written confirmed to the teacher the confusion about what was causing the movement. The teacher realised that the next step for Amanda was to consider what caused things to move or not move. This might be considered a step backwards, but it was the only way for Amanda to move forward! She spent some time making things move and stopping them and talking about what caused these changes.

It is not only when children make statements which are inconsistent with scientific concepts that their ideas are the basis for deciding next steps. For example, after collecting a variety of different 'minibeasts' some 11 year olds tried to keep them in their classroom. After some disasters they returned a number to where they had found them. But they were successful with their 'snailery'. The snails were observed for several weeks and they laid eggs, which the children took as a sign that the snails were being well cared for. During this time they investigated the snails' reaction to various conditions and foods, making a prediction about each one before trying it. For instance in the case of water they expected the snails to be attracted to it. They also tried flour, salt, sand, sawdust and oatmeal.

The predictions the children were making about whether the snails might or might not like the various things suggested to the teacher that they were linking what they had observed about the conditions in which the animals thrived to the features of the living things. This indicated readiness for a step towards ideas about adaptation of living things to particular environmental conditions. She helped them take this step initially by introducing them to animals that live in very different environments and asking them to discuss if the animals would be able to live if their habitats were exchanged and to give reasons for their answers.

Next steps for the teacher

In order to suggest in more general terms how to help the children advance their ideas we have to look at the sorts of ideas that are likely to be found. In Chapter 4 some common features of children's ideas, as revealed through research in many different contexts, were listed. As we said there, the children's ideas are based on their reasoning and experience and, although both are limited by their immaturity, these are important reasons for taking their ideas seriously.

Features of children's ideas	Helpful next steps
Attention to only one factor, ignoring others that also affect a result	Brainstorm in a group all the things that might be making a difference (different children may well have paid attention to different factors) and then 'fair test' each one
Ideas based on perception of surface similarities rather than relevant features	Investigate similarities and differences between the two things that are linked
Words used without a grasp of their scientific meaning	Ask children to give examples of what they mean by the word and supply an alternative word if necessary; take care to use words appropriately and check that the children know what they mean
Ideas based on limited experience	Extend the range of relevant experience and ensure that their ideas about it are tested
Ideas that don't fit the evidence available	Make sure that they are using process skills systematically in testing whether their ideas fit evidence
Different ideas explaining the same phenomenon in different contexts	Help them link one phenomenon to another by trying to see if the idea that explains one will also explain the other
Ideas remain unchanged in the face of contradictory evidence because no alternative available	Provide the opportunity for them to consider alternatives (for consideration but not as 'right' answers), by discussion with other pupils or with the teacher, or from books or other sources of information

Table 7.1 Ways of helping children develop their ideas

These features also give a clear indication of how to help the development of the ideas. Table 7.1 lists the common features of children's ideas and suggests some appropriate next steps. Whilst keeping these general approaches in mind it is also helpful, in planning work 'through the mind of a child', to anticipate the ideas that children are likely to have.

As an example, take planning work on soil. We need first to identify what children are likely to know about soil and the likely meanings it has for them. Here are some infants' responses to the question 'What can you tell me about soil?'

● 'It's dirt.'
● 'Seeds grow in soil.'
● 'Worms live in soil.'

● 'My dad digs it.'
● 'Our dog digs it too.'

Interestingly, some of these comments were made also in a lower-junior and an upper-junior class.

With such anticipated responses as a starting point we can consider how ideas might develop to build up a wider concept of soil. Figure 7.1 shows how one teacher attempted to map ideas in this way, starting with the anticipated response 'Worms live in soil'. Other starting ideas would produce different detail but would have a similar pattern. The advantage of planning is that it draws attention to links between statements and to what children could *do* to help make the links themselves. (For example, a useful experience would be for the children to investigate 'Which soil is easiest to tunnel through?') In this way planning for development of ideas and skills goes hand in hand.

There is no need to be put off by thinking that detailed knoweldge of soil (or any other topic) is needed. The statements in Fig. 7.1 are largely general-knowledge statements, emerging from the analysis of soil and its properties and interaction with things in it. The same strategy applies for any topic and can be summarised as:

1. Identify children's likely knowledge and meanings.
2. Map a possible development of ideas.
3. Consider what experience children need to link one idea to another.

The teacher's role

Looking back across Table 7.1, there are several key aspects of the teacher's role in helping children to develop their ideas. These are:

1. *To provide opportunities for practical activities*, for two main purposes:

● extending children's experiences;

● enabling children to test out their ideas.

2. *To provide opportunities for discussion*, which may at different times:

● facilitate the linking of ideas in one context to related happenings in another;

● clarify the meaning of words used;

● enable different ideas to be exchanged and shared;

● aid recognition that others may have a different interpretation of shared experiences;

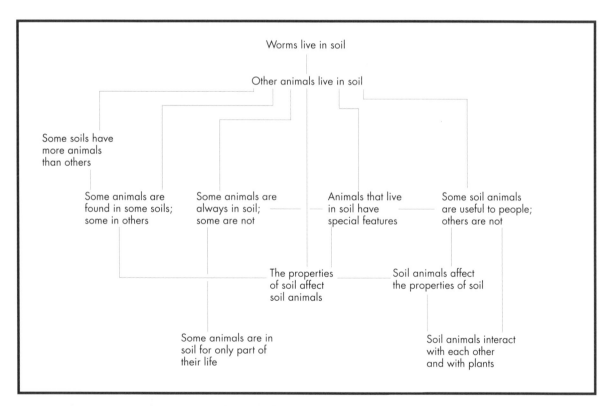

Fig. 7.1 Planning part of a soil topic 'through the mind of a child'

- help realise the need for evidence to support a point of view.

3. *To provide access to information and ideas* for children to use in helping to make sense of their experiences, particularly in relation to:

- events and objects that they cannot explore at first hand (sun, stars and space, for example);

- alternative ideas that they can compare with their own when testing them against evidence;

- information about how to use equipment (e.g. microscopes and thermometers) and about how to stay safe when investigating.

4. *To provide opportunities and incentives for children to communicate* their ideas so that they:

- clarify their own understanding through talking or writing;

- have the opportunity to explain their ideas to others and to listen to others' explanations.

Discussion is so important that perhaps the final word should be about the teacher's role in encouraging it. Discussion does not just happen. To ensure that it has its full value, action is needed on two fronts.

- Teachers need to monitor their responses to children's contributions. How often, feeling pressed for time and over-keen to get on with what they have planned, do teachers respond with a semi-dismissive 'y-e-s' and quickly draw in someone else? Children are not slow to pick up the implied irrelevance of their contribution and they may be less forthcoming in future.

- Teachers must make sure that children have the chance to acquire the necessary confidence and skills to engage in discussion. This may require conscious development as part of an oral language programme.

8

USING ASSESSMENT TO HELP DEVELOPMENT OF PROCESS SKILLS AND ATTITUDES

Chapter 7 was concerned with children's ideas and how to use assessment to help this aspect of their learning. Now we turn to consider the development of skills and attitudes, recognising that this part of learning in science cannot be separated from the development of ideas. The frequent references in Chapter 7 to the use of skills to test ideas and the importance of doing this systematically underline this point.

Skills and attitudes are being used in all investigative work. Thus the opportunities to find out how they are being used and what development is needed are frequently present in children's work. This is in contrast with the ideas about particular subject matter, which clearly have to be assessed and developed when that subject matter is being studied. (We can't assess ideas about electricity when dealing with why leaves fall off trees!)

So in suggesting how skills and attitudes might be assessed as part of teaching, we again propose things that teachers can try out to become familiar with how this can be done, but in this case it can be done during any investigative work going on in the classroom – perhaps even the fabrics-testing activity in Chapter 2, or any similar activity that will enable children to use their investigative skills.

An approach to assessing skills and attitudes as part of teaching

This approach to assessing skills and attitudes depends on the notion that these aspects of behaviour develop during the primary years from less mature to the more mature forms that are required

for secondary science. However we recognise that the use of process skills is influenced by what the children use the skills on. The subject matter has to be within the grasp of the children's understanding. For example, a child of 9 who can suggest a 'fair test' for which of several balls is bounciest is probably not able to suggest a fair test of which of several solutions has the highest osmotic pressure. So judgements about process skills must be made in the context of investigations in which the ideas being tested are the children's own or ones that they are capable of understanding.

In the following pages are sets of questions about things children may or may not be able to do relating to the following science skills and attitudes:

Science process skills	Scientific attitudes
Observing	Willingness to collect and use evidence (respect for evidence)
Explaining (hypothesising)	
Predicting	Willingness to change ideas in the light of evidence (flexibility)
Raising questions	
Planning and conducting investigations	
Interpreting	Willingness to review procedures critically (critical reflection)
Communicating	

Table 8.1 Process skills and attitudes

The questions early in the checklists below concern things that are likely to be developed sooner than those further down in the lists, but this is only a rough guide to development and there will be many different patterns in individual progress.

We suggest the following procedure for the first time that these questions are used.

1. Read through the descriptions of development and the questions that follow for the process skills and attitudes.
2. Choose one group of children to observe throughout an extended period of activity in which the skills are likely to be used. The idea is for the teacher to interact normally with all groups but to pay particular attention to the selected group in relation to the questions in the lists.
3. Note (mentally and on paper when there is time, but *not* using the list as a checklist on a clip board!) any evidence that relates to the development of skills and attitudes.
4. At a later time, after the lesson, look through the questions and consider if there is evidence that enables each to be answered by 'yes' or 'no'. Of course there won't be evidence for a decision on all questions and where there was no opportunity for the observation to be made these should be recorded as 'not applicable'.
5. Although it won't be possible to be definite about each question there is likely to be a point in each list where the answers stop being a firm 'yes' and gradually change into 'no'. Try to identify this region of development.
6. This procedure will probably be more difficult for some lists than for others. This shouldn't be a cause of worry; indeed it might be best to begin with a reduced list of those skills more likely to be used in all activities (observing, predicting, communicating) and return to the others later.

Assessing skills

Observing

This is the skill of taking in information about all the things around. It can, and should at various times, involve the use of all the senses. Development in observation has two aspects which at first seem conflicting; on the one hand the increasing ability to notice as much detail as possible and not be limited by what one expects to find, and on the other hand the increasing ability to distinguish between what is relevant to a particular problem and what is not. There is a danger in narrowing the focus of observation too soon to what is regarded as relevant. This is a long-term aim and priority at the primary level should be given to attention to detail and sequence.

Do the children:

- succeed in identifying obvious differences and similarities between objects and materials?

- make use of several senses in exploring objects or materials?

- identify differences of detail between objects or materials?

- identify points of similarity between objects where differences are more obvious than similarities?

- use their senses appropriately and extend the range of sight using a hand lens or microscope as necessary?

- notice patterns, relationships or sequences that are to be found in a series of observations?

- distinguish from many observations those which are relevant to the problem in hand?

Explaining (hypothesising)

The skill of explaining something involves using previous experience and existing ideas. The ideas which are applied are selected because of some similarity between the new event or objects and those encountered previously.

Some of children's explanations are no more than statements of coincident circumstances; others take the form of labels (as if giving something a name explains it – typically, a word such as 'energy' is used in this way). More advanced explanations are in terms of mechanisms, but of course there is always a further question to be asked about any explanation. (See Chapter 10 for some discussion of the levels of explanation appropriate at the primary level.)

Do the children:

- attempt to give an explanation which is consistent with evidence, even if only in terms of the presence of certain features or circumstances?

- attempt to explain things in terms of a relevant idea from previous experience even if they go no further than naming it?

- suggest not only what but how something is brought about, even if the 'how' would be difficult to check?

- show awareness that there may be more than one explanation which fits the evidence?

- give explanations which suggest how an observed effect or situation is brought about and which could be checked?

- show awareness that all explanations are tentative and never proved beyond doubt?

Predicting

Making a prediction goes beyond the evidence which has been gathered and uses what is available to suggest what will happen after some process has continued or changes have been made. The use of evidence or previous experience distinguishes a prediction from a guess, which does not appear to have a rational basis.

There are various degrees of using evidence, which signify levels of sophistication in using this skill. At the lower levels, children tend to jump to conclusions, which have only a slight link with the evidence. At a rather more advanced level the link is firmer but perhaps still intuitive. Later still comes the ability to explain how the evidence is used in arriving at the prediction by some form of extrapolation or interpolation.

Do the children:

- attempt to make a prediction relating to a problem even if it is not derived from the evidence?

- make some use of evidence in making a prediction, rather than basing it on preconceived ideas?

- make reasonable predictions which fit the evidence without necessarily being able to make the justification explicit?

- explain how evidence has been used in making predictions?

- perceive and use patterns in information or observations to make justified interpolations or extrapolations?

- show caution in making assumptions about the generalisation of patterns beyond the evidence available?

Raising questions

Whilst we are concerned here with questions of a particular kind, we do not want to imply that these are the only worthwhile questions. Children should be encouraged to ask all kinds of questions, since it is through doing this that they can help form links between previous and new experience and so enlarge their understanding. In science, however, we are concerned with questions which can be investigated, that children can answer through action – action which involves the science process skills.

Fundamental to the development of the skill of raising investigable questions is the gradual recognition of the kind of question with which science is concerned. This is basic to the appreciation of scientific activity. Beyond the primary years the pupils may learn to recognise some questions as philosophical, others as essentially matters of value or of aesthetic judgement. In the primary years, however, the distinction is between those which cannot be answered through scientific enquiry (e.g. why does someone prefer one pattern of wallpaper to another?) and those which can if they are expressed in certain ways (e.g. which fabric is best for making a raincoat? – this is testable when we have decided what 'best' means and how to test it).

Do the children:

- readily ask a variety of questions which include investigable and non-investigable ones?

- recognise a difference between an investigable question and one which cannot be answered by investigation?

- realise when an investigable question is in a testable form?

- generally, in science, ask questions which are potentially investigable?

- quite often express their own questions in testable form?

- ask questions which arise from making a prediction or giving an explanation that can be tested?

Planning and conducting investigations

What is involved here is both planning and carrying out a series of actions which are related to finding an answer to a particular question. It will generally involve action to change something and then observing the effect of the change whilst other things are kept the same; or it may involve comparing different things when treated in the same way. Key features are: selecting the appropriate variable to change or objects to compare, keeping all other things the same (controlling variables), and observing or measuring the relevant effect systematically and carefully.

Children at the early levels of this skill have to 'think as they go' in their investigations; those at more advanced levels will be able to plan ahead before starting an investigation, to anticipate what is involved and take action to avoid possible problems.

Do the children:

- start with a useful general approach even if details are lacking or need further thought?

- have some ideas of the variable that has to be changed or what different things are to be compared?

- keep the same those things which should not change for a fair test?

- have some ideas beforehand of what to look for to obtain a result?

- choose a realistic way of measuring or comparing things to obtain the results?

- take steps to ensure that the results obtained are as accurate as they can reasonably be?

Interpreting

Once children have obtained some results or observations it is important that they use them and go beyond the mere collection of data. They should return to their original questions and try to answer them from the results of the investigation. This may involve looking for patterns in the results – were the changes they made in one variable followed by change in some other variable (change in the temperature of the water and change in the speed of dissolving)? Or there may be associations between a set of circumstances and a certain result (the healthy growth of a plant and the conditions in which it was grown).

At early stages children tend to look at individual findings rather than at the combined meaning of all their results. They may say that 'the heaviest went furthest' rather than 'the heavier the load the further it went', thus combining all their results. Development is shown by an increasing ability to draw conclusions which summarise and are consistent with the evidence but at the same time realising that the conclusions may not apply beyond the evidence collected.

Do the children:

- discuss what they find in relation to their initial questions?

- compare their findings with their earlier predictions?

- notice associations between changes in one variable and another?

- identify patterns or trends in their results?

- check any patterns or trends against all the evidence?

- draw conclusions which summarise and are consistent with the evidence?

- recognise that any conclusions may have to be changed in the light of new evidence?

Communicating

This is the skill of giving others, as clearly as possible, an indication of ideas and evidence used in and arising from an investigation. It also involves receiving, understanding and responding to information given by others.

Informal communication, both written and spoken, is a means of sorting out ideas and linking different experiences to each other. Formal communication skills are quite heavily dependent on the knowledge of conventions, such as names of objects or events, how to draw graphs, tables, charts and use symbols. Development in communication skills doesn't just reside in knowing the conventions, but rather in the appropriate use of the various means of communication to suit the receivers and the type of information.

Do the children:

- talk freely about their activities and the ideas they have, with or without making a written record?

- listen to others' ideas and look at their results?

- report events coherently in drawings, writing, models, paintings?

- use tables, graphs and charts to record and report results when these are suggested?

- regularly and spontaneously use information books to check or supplement their investigations?

- choose a form for recording or presenting results which is both considered and justified?

Assessing attitudes

Attitudes are distinct from skills and concepts in that they describe the willingness to act or react in a certain way, whilst skills and concepts describe the required know-how to do so. However, it is clear that in practice these three are much less distinct, for, on the one hand, we can't really be predisposed to use a skill or idea that we don't possess, on the other hand, there must be some willingness to use the skill or concept in order to develop it at all.

It is useful, though, to regard attitudes as separable from skills and concepts to some degree. It helps us pay particular attention to them and reminds us that not only do we need to teach children so that they *can* use scientific skills and ideas but also so that they *will* use them to work scientifically.

Attitudes are 'caught' as much as 'taught'; they are encouraged most effectively in children by a mixture of example and approval of the behaviour they describe. So, to foster respect for evidence, flexibility of ideas and critical thinking in our children, the best way is to show these attitudes in our own behaviour.

Willingness to collect and use evidence (respect for evidence)

Do the children:

- report results which are supported by evidence even if the interpretation is influenced by preconceived ideas?

- realise when the evidence doesn't fit a conclusion based on expectations, although they may challenge the evidence rather than the conclusion?

- check parts of the evidence which don't fit an overall pattern or conclusions?

- accept only interpretations or conclusions for which there is supporting evidence?

- show a desire to collect further evidence to check conclusions before accepting them?

- recognise that no conclusion is so firm that it can't be challenged by further evidence?

Willingness to change ideas in the light of evidence (flexibility)

Do the children:

- readily change what they say they think, though this may be due to a desire to please rather than the force of argument or evidence?

- change ideas when there is considerable evidence against the existing ones and little in their favour?

- show willingness to consider alternative ideas which may fit the evidence, even if they prefer their own in the end?

- relinquish or change ideas after considering evidence?

- spontaneously seek other ideas which may fit the evidence rather than accepting the first which seems to fit?

- recognise that ideas can be changed by thinking and reflecting about different ways of making sense of the same evidence?

Willingness to review procedures critically (critical reflection)

Do the children:

- review what they have done after an investigation even though they may only justify rather than criticise it?

- consider some alternative procedures which could have been used without necessarily realising their advantages and disadvantages?

- discuss ways in which what they have done could have been improved even if only in detail?

- consider, when encouraged, the pros and cons of alternative ways of approaching a problem to the one they have used?

- initiate review of a completed investigation to identify how procedures could have been improved?

- spontaneously review and improve procedures at the planning stage and in the course of an investigation as well as after completion?

Using the information to encourage development of skills and attitudes

Deciding the next steps for the children

1. The points in the checklists where 'yes' answers turn into 'no' answers or where there are 'yes/no' answers indicate the areas of advancement. Having identified these the teacher should pay particular attention to them, and:

   - listen and watch how the children tackle the relevant part of their investigation;

   - ask the children to talk through this part of the investigation to find out their view of what it involves;

   - discuss the problems they have in tackling this part and suggest alternatives to them;

   - decide on the basis of their responses whether they are on the point of the change which is required or whether more practice and consolidation at an earlier point of development is appropriate.

2. Children should be given the opportunity and encouragement to try those things next down on the lists, where they do not yet succeed. This is best done within activities where the subject matter is familiar and non-threatening (i.e. not in an activity which involves using equipment never used before, but perhaps in extending investigations using already familiar materials).

3. At the same time there should be plenty of opportunity for children to do the things they can do (the 'yes' answers) so that their confidence is maintained.

4. Children should be encouraged, as a routine, to critically review how activities have been carried out, so that they realise the skills they need.

Next steps for the teacher

1. This approach has been discussed in terms of observing groups of children. For many purposes of using the information in teaching, this is sufficient. But there will also be the need to consider individual children. Increasing familiarity with the questions in the checklists and with the development they describe enables teachers to carry this knowledge around in their heads. They are then be able to use it in noticing how individual children go about their work.

2. The importance of children having opportunity to use and develop process skills means that it is essential for the teacher to be constantly vigilant about providing these opportunities. The assessment of children has implications for self-assessment by teachers. It is worthwhile, therefore, for teachers to check systematically that, over a reasonable period of time, there is evidence for making a decision about the questions on each checklist. If this evidence is not available – if 'not applicable' appears as a regular response – it may be that the opportunities of the child in relation to a skill or attitude are rather limited. Then it may help to revisit Chapter 3 and review the children's activities.

9

USING ASSESSMENT TO SUMMARISE PROGRESS

What was described in the last two chapters may not have been recognised as assessment since it doesn't fit the common view that assessment is a rather more formal process, ending in some kind of grade or mark. This chapter puts the activities in Chapters 7 and 8 in the context of the wide range of activities that come under the broad definition of assessment.

We also consider the various purposes of assessment and emphasise that different approaches to assessment are needed to serve these purposes. It is important to keep the specific purposes in mind when considering what information is to be collected, and how it is collected and used.

Although the points made here are rather more theoretical than the discussion of assessment in the previous chapters, we feel that they are helpful in ensuring that assessment has a positive role in education. The old adage that 'the assessment tail can wag the curriculum dog' indicates the negative side of assessment; teaching restricted by what is assessed. The positive side is that, as we have tried to show in Chapters 7 and 8, assessment is essential to teaching that aims to bring about progressive understanding. However, if this positive role is to be preserved then assessment for this purpose must not be confused with what is necessary to serve other, different, purposes.

Meanings and purposes of assessment

The most general statement about the meaning of assessment is that it is a process which involves:

● gathering information about aspects of behaviour or achievement; and

● making some judgement of this information by comparing it with a standard or expectation.

The outcome of this process is a judgement and the actual behaviour is replaced by this judgement. What this means is that assessment is not the same as description, nor a recording of everything that happens. Just what form the outcome takes and what use is made of it depends crucially on the purposes of the assessment. So let's look at what the purposes can be.

Although long lists of purposes of assessment can be created, they can be comfortably grouped under five headings, namely those relating to:

1. *Teaching individual children*:
   ● finding out children's ideas and skills as starting points;
   ● identifying problems and next steps;
   ● supporting progression in learning.
2. *Identifying where children have reached at certain points*:
   ● reporting achievements to parents, to other teachers and to children themselves;
   ● assisting forward planning of future work.
3. *Certification and awards*:
   ● indicating the achievement of individuals in a publicly recognised way.
4. *School evaluation*:
   ● enabling teachers to reflect upon how effective their teaching has been;
   ● contributing to school self-evaluation aimed at identifying areas for development planning;
   ● providing information to those outside the school to judge its effectiveness (hopefully as part of a much wider range of information needed for this purposes).

5. *Monitoring and research*:
- providing information about achievement nationally or regionally;
- enabling the achievement of sub-groups to be compared;
- providing information for evaluating new teaching methods, materials and organisations.

Items 1–3 in this list are concerned with the performance of individual children and the information will affect them directly in either the short-term or the long-term. Items 4 and 5 deal with the performance of groups of children and will not directly affect the future of individual children. All are necessary and important purposes, although for several purposes the information about pupils' achievement is not sufficient on its own.

Our concern here is with the first two purposes because assessment for both these purposes is carried out by teachers and is an important part of their work.

The first is what we have discussed in Chapters 7 and 8. It is usually described as formative or diagnostic assessment; it is also known as developmental assessment (Masters and Forster, 1996). As we have seen, this is concerned with on-going teaching and becomes part of it.

Assessment for the second kind of purpose is known as summative assessment. This differs from formative assessment in several respects, particularly because it is carried out at certain intervals rather than at any time and it is used to summarise achievement over a period of time rather than being concerned with specific learning activities.

The features of formative and summative assessment

We now look at some other ways in which these kinds of assessment differ and which it is important to recognise if both are to be used effectively and efficiently for their intended purposes.

Type of information

Because formative assessment is carried out so that it can be used in helping teaching and learning, the type of information it requires is concerned with the learning in the activities as they take place. It will therefore concern the ideas and skills that can be developed in particular activities. We can call these 'small' ideas because they are likely to be specific to the activity. Of course the teacher will have in mind 'bigger' ideas, of wider application, towards which he or she intends the children to make progress. Several 'small' ideas will have to be linked together to form gradually bigger and bigger ideas. (There is more discussion of this in Chapter 10.)

For example, the children collecting 'minibeasts' and attempting to keep them in their classroom (page 49) were learning about the conditions needed for survival by the particular animals that they found. Their teacher would want them to link their ideas about these particular creatures to their experiences with other living things – keeping pets, learning about animals in the wild, etc. – in order to form general ideas about the needs of living things and eventually to link the characteristics of animals to the features of the habitats in which they live. The characteristics of living things and adaptation to habitat are 'big' ideas (big because they relate to more than the particular animals studied) that will become bigger still as children's experience extends and supports a deeper understanding of these concepts.

Summative assessment is concerned with progress towards the big ideas rather than the learning in specific activities. For this the teacher will wish to judge the extent to which the children can apply ideas in different contexts other than those of the activities in which they were learned.

Comparability of outcomes

Formative and summative assessment also differ in the way information about aspects of children's behaviour is judged. As we noted on page 60 assessment always involves a judgement and the outcome is the product of the judgement. The outcome may be a mark, grade or comment or even a smile or a frown. But how does a teacher (or anyone else involved in assessment) decide what is acceptable, what deserves special praise or what should be regarded as 'not up to standard'. The word 'standard' gives a clue, for there is always something – a standard – against which the judgement is made. There are three kinds of standard in common use in assessment:

- expectations based on knowledge of a particular child (the result is described as child-referenced assessment);

- specified aspects or levels of achievement (criterion-referenced assessment);

- the average or 'norm' for the group of which the child is a member (norm-referenced assessment).

In formative assessment teachers are interested in the progress made by individuals and how to help further achievement, which means that in deciding whether the smile or the frown is the appropriate response, the teacher will take into account the child's previous achievement, the effort put in and any particular difficulties the child is experiencing, as well as the quality of the work. This means that it is possible that a piece of work which might result in praise for one child would, if produced by another, be regarded as less than satisfactory for that other child. There is no harm in this *as long as comparisons between children are not made on the basis of these assessments*. What the teacher is doing is using a mixture of child-referenced and criterion-referenced assessment. This is good practice, since, if the teacher were to use strictly criterion-referenced assessment, the same for all the children, then for some this would mean constant discouragement.

For summative assessment, however, it is important *that comparable outcomes of assessment imply comparable quality of work*. So the grades, levels, marks, and so on that are assigned to children's work must mean the same thing for different children. Their meaning comes from the criteria being applied. For this purpose, then, no aspects should be considered other than what the work means in terms of ideas and skills achieved.

The danger of mixing these two purposes of assessment are obvious. Children given good marks, as encouragement, might suddenly find that their end-of-session assessment is much less encouraging. It is, therefore, essential for teachers to ensure that there is a clear distinction between the two, both in their minds and the children's. One way of doing this is to take care that marks are only given where they are useful and that they are always comparable from one child to another, that is, that they are outcomes of criterion-referenced assessment. Formative assessment is not concerned with marks, grades and levels; its outcomes are comments, questions and suggestions that promote learning.

The role of the children

Encouraging children to take part in the assessment of their own work is a way in which teachers can communicate to children the objectives of their learning. When children share some understanding of where they are going in their learning they can take a more active part in deciding their next steps and have greater commitment to taking these steps. Teacher and children then work together and can discuss the best way to overcome difficulties and develop ideas and skills.

The children's role in assessment is most readily encouraged in the context of assessing specific pieces of work. Creating portfolios, or collections of work in folders or boxes, is a popular and effective way of doing this. The children might be asked to select from their collection the pieces of work they think are the best. In discussion with the teacher the child explains why the particular pieces of work were chosen and this gives an indication of what the child values and strives for. This may or may not coincide with the teacher's concept of what is good work. For instance, in science the teacher will be looking for behaviours described in the checklists of questions in Chapter 8 whilst the child may pick out work for its neatness and careful handwriting. Without discouraging good writing, the teacher can pick out other pieces of work and praise evidence of the kinds of skills, attitudes and ideas that he or she is aiming to foster ('I like what you wrote here because …' or 'this drawing was a good way of showing your ideas about …'). This helps the child to share, through concrete examples, the teacher's objectives.

Reviewing work in this way gives the children opportunity to assess and help direct their future work and so has a role in formative assessment. The extent to which primary children can genuinely take part in summative assessment is limited. This requires understanding of rather longer-term aims and the broader picture of the progression in learning, as well as the ability to stand aside from their work that will develop at a later stage.

Summarising progress

Table 9.1 summarises the features of formative and summative assessment which have been discussed. The table emphasises the differences, although in practice things are not so clear cut; rather than two distinctly different kinds of assessment there is more of a continuum from formative to summative. There are also similarities:

- both kinds address the same learning objectives, one in the context of specific activities, the other in terms of more general application of skills and ideas;

- they must both cover the whole range of these objectives: all the skills, attitudes and ideas that are the concern of education;

- they are both conducted by the teacher.

It follows that much of the information gathered for formative purposes can be used for summative purposes. Indeed it should be, since it is the richest source of information about the children's achievement. But for dependable assessment, as required

Feature	Formative/diagnostic	Summative
Purpose	Helping teaching; promoting learning; positive in intent	Reporting achievement at certain points in time, usually at 'natural breaks'
Timing	Takes place as an on-going part of teaching	Takes place at specified times
Use	As basis for 'next steps' in learning	Report to parents, other teachers and pupil on point reached in learning
Type of evidence	About ideas ('small' ideas) and skills used in particular activities and how these were arrived at	About the grasp of 'bigger' ideas which are achieved as a result of several activities and which relate to the requirements of the curriculum
Basis of judgements	Takes account of effort as well as quality of work	Takes account of the quality of the work only
Comparability of judgements	Judgement depends on the child as well as the criteria; so not comparable for different children	Products of assessment (grades, levels, marks, etc.) mean the same for all children
Role of children	Children have a central part in the assessment of their own work	Children have a part but there must be overall confidence that criteria are applied in the same way for all children

Table 9.1 The different features of formative and summative assessment

for summative purposes, there must be certain conditions on the use of this information, specifically that:

- it is reviewed strictly against the criteria;

- the criteria are applied in a 'best fit' approach;

- there is some way of ensuring that the judgements of one teacher are comparable with those of other teachers.

We need to look at what these points mean in practice.

Reviewing achievement against criteria

The feedback to children in formative assessment, as we have seen, takes account of their individual progress, their effort and any special circumstances affecting particular activities. For summative purposes, however, it is important to consider what the children have actually done, what they have achieved in relation to the learning intended for all children (usually specified in a curriculum statement such as the National Curriculum). So the work has to be reviewed with these common criteria in mind.

Applying criteria in a 'best fit' approach

Children's work over a period of time will show peaks and troughs. At times they may seem to be able to do something which at other times they seem unable to do. These ups and downs are useful for formative purposes because they indicate conditions which work in favour of or against certain kinds of achievement.

But for summative purposes they pose a difficulty for the decision as to whether or not a child has achieved a particular level in skills or understanding. So the technique is to review the work as a whole and to decide the 'best fit' with the criteria to be applied, accepting that not every piece of work will meet the criteria and not every criterion will be met.

Professional judgement is required and this can be enhanced by teachers having opportunity to discuss together actual collections of children's work and sharing their views on how they should be assessed.

Ensuring judgements are comparable

One way of ensuring that judgements made by different teachers for summative purposes are comparable is to provide opportunities of the kind just described, where teachers meet to compare their judgements. Another way is to build up a bank of exemplars that can be used as reference points in making judgement. The publication of such exemplars has been a useful aid in helping teachers in England and Wales conduct the assessment required for National Curriculum Assessment.

A third way is to provide a means for teachers to check their own assessments by using an externally devised task or test that has been validated for the purpose of indicating certain levels of achievement. This is what is done in Scotland, where national tests are available (only in reading, writing and mathematics) for teachers to use to confirm their judgements as to when children have achieved a certain level. In England and Wales the non-statutory tests for areas of the curriculum not covered by statutory testing serve a similar purpose.

The role of special tasks

We noted earlier that the kind of information needed for summative assessment concerns development of 'bigger' ideas and the ability to apply ideas in contexts other than those in which they were learned. This means that summarising evidence from learning activities carried out may not provide all the information that is needed to report on progress. True, some information about ability to apply ideas will be gained as an on-going part of teaching and this will contribute to summative assessment. However, in addition to using information from learning activities, there may be the need to introduce tasks designed to assess understanding, through application of ideas, and the ability to use skills in a range of contexts.

It is also the case that, more and more, teachers are being required to report performance against specified criteria in curriculum statements. Thus it is helpful to have some information about performance that can be easily related to these statements and/or criteria for levels of achievement.

We are not suggesting formal tests but rather that teachers introduce tasks chosen to provide information needed to supplement what they already have from the on-going activities. These tasks need not be externally produced and indeed the main value of ones that are available from publications is to give ideas to teachers to develop their own. Examples of useful approaches are:

1. *Using a themed set of questions* in which children can be asked to write their ideas for planning investigations, how to interpret given data, how to explain some findings that are described, etc. An example is the set of tasks on the theme of 'The Walled Garden' (Schilling et al., 1990), which provide materials for teachers to introduce to children as a topic or a story, with sections on leaves, minibeasts, bark, wood, walls, water, leaves and a sundial, and questions designed to require the use of process skills in this range of topics.

2. *Using concept maps* to explore children's understanding of links between things. Concept maps are diagrammatic ways of representing relationships between words. For example the map in Fig. 9.1 (from Harlen, 1996) was drawn by 6 year old Lennie, using words relating to his ideas about heat and its effects on various

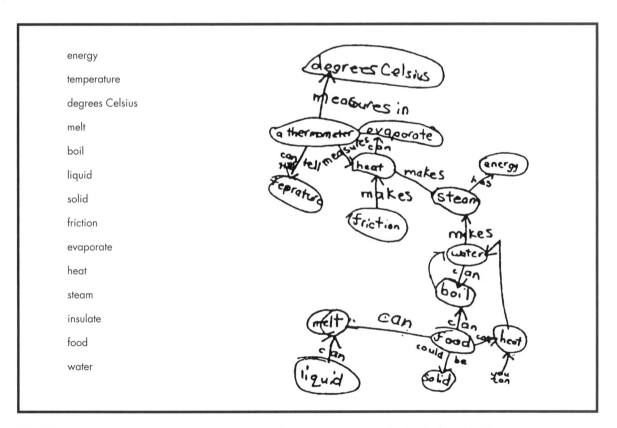

Fig. 9.1   A concept map (from *The Teaching of Science in Primary Schools*, Harlen, 1996)

things. The words were supplied by the teacher and were ones that she knew Lennie had encountered. Some teachers write the words on cards, so that the children can move them around while they are thinking about how they are related to each other, and then draw the arrows and the words that link them. Reading the maps produced in this way helps a teacher to know what ideas have been formed. For example, Lennie has some useful ideas about the effects of heat but has not distinguished heat from temperature.

3. *Developing a 'circus' of small practical tasks* designed to address particular criteria. These can be open-ended so that the level of achievement is determined from the response, or more targeted at a particular level. Introduced as part of their work, children invariably enjoy the change and challenge that these activities provide. As well as providing the additional information that teachers need to report on progress, they also give a great deal of information that can be used in planning later topics and activities.

In this final chapter we look back over some issues already raised to take them further and we look forward at some new ones. The title deliberately echoes that of Chapter 1 where we focused on learning science. Subsequent chapters have addressed ways of bringing about the kind of learning described there. We did not at that stage say much about the view of science that was implied. This is something we now take up briefly in the first part of this chapter. We then continue the discussion of learning and consider how 'small' ideas are turned into 'bigger' ones, or more widely applicable concepts. This brings us to the questions of which big ideas we should be aiming to develop in the primary years and how 'big' they should be. Finally we look at the vexed question of primary teachers' own understanding of science and consider again the teacher's role in bringing about learning with understanding.

Significance of the view of science

In Chapter 4 we suggested that decisions about teaching start from a view of learning, that is, the understanding of what it is to learn and how learning is brought about. Now we want to add that a view of *what is to be learned* has a part in these decisions. If a teacher has a view of science as being concerned with facts, figures and laws, then not only is this likely to be seen as less than enthralling, but teaching it will be regarded as essentially the transmission of this body of knowledge. Yes, there will be some practical work, but this will serve to illustrate and verify what the children have been told rather than being a means of learning it.

This view of science as knowledge which, in a sense, already exists in that it has been 'proved to be true', also involves regarding science as objective and value-free. Such a view is not surprising among those whose experience of secondary schools science was of an over-loaded syllabus, where facts had to be memorised and laws proved, with too little opportunity for building up understanding.

But this is out of step with the modern view of science as being the creation of human minds and actions, from which come ideas and relationships that are regarded as always open to challenge and change in the light of further evidence. The human element in science, including the constraining role of values, is recognised. This makes science exciting and accessible to everyone and not just to those who can succeed in absorbing a multitude of facts and abstract relationships. In this view of science, the development of ideas is seen, in fact, in rather the same as way we have described the learning of science; starting from previous knowledge and understanding and building on it, not accepting it uncritically but always putting it to the test of whether it helps the understanding of new experience.

We can easily see that holding the first of these views of science, as established facts, would tend to lead to teachers wanting to ensure that the knowledge of past generations is passed on as accurately as possible to new generations. Holding the second view of science, as current understandings that are always open to change, would mean that learners should understand how scientific knowledge is created. The best way of doing this is to involve them in it. If we add to this a commitment to children learning with understanding, as described in Chapter 4, then we have a firm theoretical foundation for the approach adopted in this book.

Development of 'big' ideas

It is worthwhile recalling at this point the main features of the view of learning that we have described, emphasising the relationship between processes and concepts, since, in the subsequent discussion of ideas, we do not want the role of processes to be lost.

- Children will already have some ideas or concepts which they bring to a new experience in trying to understand it. Thus learning involves change in ideas, not creating them from scratch.

- Ideas change and develop by being checked against evidence from new experiences. The checking involves the processes of observing, explaining, predicting, investigating, etc.

- How the processing is done has a profound influence on the emerging ideas; process skills have an important role in concept development.

These points reiterate something about the mechanism of change, but they do not tell us what sorts of change are taking place. Is there a pattern in children's changing ideas? How do the concepts of a typical 6 year old differ from those of a typical 10 year old?

There certainly are patterns in the development of ideas and it is useful to know them, as long as we resist the temptation to say that because a child is *x* years old then she or he 'ought' to have these kinds of ideas rather than those.

The two most helpful patterns to have in mind concern the *range* and the *degree of abstraction* of ideas.

Development of the range of ideas

What we find is that:

1. The ideas of young children are limited to a few objects or events; they are what we have called 'small' ideas ('what I eat for breakfast' and 'what I eat for dinner'; 'this toy lorry rolls down the slope'; 'when I put this substance in water it disappears').
2. Gradually the small ideas become linked up into bigger ideas encompassing a wider range of instances ('things I eat'; 'the higher the slope the further the lorry rolls'; 'some things disappear in water and others don't').
3. The process of merging continues so that even bigger ideas are formed ('food'; 'forces make things move'; 'dissolving').

We might represent the process as shown in Fig. 10.1.

If only small ideas are available, there is less chance of new experience fitting in than if the bigger ideas exist. For instance, the concept of food is more likely to help explain what is happening

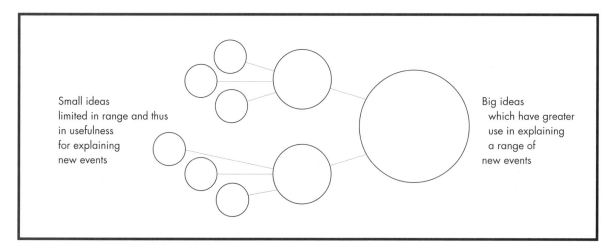

Small ideas
limited in range and thus
in usefulness
for explaining
new events

Big ideas
which have greater
use in explaining
a range of
new events

Fig. 10.1 Linkage of small ideas to become bigger ideas

when a thrush is seen consuming a snail, than a concept of 'what I eat for breakfast'. So bigger ideas have greater power in helping to explain new experience. This is why we have emphasised (Chapter 7) that teaching should aim to:

- help children to make links between ideas they already have, but may keep distinct;
- broaden the range of their ideas for applying them to new experience and making the necessary changes to accommodate it.

Development of the degree of abstraction of ideas

The pattern here indicates that:

1. Young children's small ideas are related to what is immediately observable to the senses ('strong things like bridges are made of strong materials like stone, brick and cement').
2. Gradually they are able to generalise about relationships between things ('strength depends on the way a structure like a bridge is built as well as the materials used').
3. Ideas become related to more abstract qualities ('structure/function relationship').

This sequence indicates a change in the nature of the entities which are related together in an idea or concept. To be able to deal with abstract qualities requires a great deal of experience of dealing with concrete things and forming generalisations about them, and the general mental ability for abstract thought. Children in the primary years, by and large, do not reach the point of being able to use and develop concepts at a high level of abstraction. They can, however, be helped to consider the way things behave, not just what they are, and to begin to categorise things in terms of relationships.

A note on ideas and concepts

In this discussion, and indeed throughout the book, we have used the word 'idea' rather than 'concept' although sometimes they have been used interchangeably. Ideas can be regarded as the building blocks of concepts (Harlen, 1993) but there is such a blurred line between the two that we prefer not to try to distinguish them in the present context. Nevertheless since the words are used in much discussion of learning we must be clear about the meaning and function in learning of concepts/ideas.

- *Concepts are generalisations of some kind concerning the similar features of different objects or events.*

For instance, if we have a concept of 'chair', then on entering a room for the first time we recognise certain objects in it as chairs even though we may never have seen chairs of that shape and design before. The 'chair concept' comprises the essential qualities which are the same for all chairs and enables us to focus on certain 'chair' properties and ignore other features in classifying the objects.

- *Concepts enable us to use past experience in dealing with new experience.*

We couldn't cope with everyday life without this ability – every object and event would present an overwhelming overload to our senses.

Concepts which relate together a wide range of different phenomena are generally described as 'high-level' and tend to be more abstract. Those which have a restricted range are 'low-level' and are more concrete. For example the concepts of money, coins, and currency that we use daily can be put in order from high to low: currency, money, coins.

Science concepts are a sub-set of all concepts.

- *Science concepts are those generalisations which help us to understand the order in the natural and physical world around.*

They concern the patterns that can be discerned in the way things behave and in materials. Like all other concepts they can differ in range and degree of abstraction. Also, like other concepts, they sometimes take the form of a single word, such as:

animal	sound	dissolving
plant	reflection	floating

or sometimes the form of a relationship for which there is no single word, for example 'Whenever there is a sound there is something vibrating' or 'A complete circuit of conducting material is needed for an electric current to flow'.

Care is needed when dealing with single-word concepts, for two reasons:

1. The label, i.e. the word, cannot be found from investigation; it has to be taught. But knowing it doesn't necessarily indicate that for a child the word brings with it the full meaning that it has for an adult. The word 'animal' is an example; at first it is used by children to mean only furry, four-legged mammals, not including fish, worms, spiders, etc. Later the word will take on a wider meaning.
2. There are various levels at which a concept can be understood (as noted in Chapter 1) and the use of a single word cannot distinguish one from another and so can easily be misunderstood. For example, think of the different things that the word 'dissolving' means if you consider the ideas of the 6 year old, the 16 year old and the 26 year old research chemist.

In this discussion we could have added '. . . or idea' each time the work 'concept' was used. Low-level concepts would be 'small ideas' and high-level concepts would be 'big ideas'. But there is one important difference, which leads to a preference for using 'ideas' rather than concepts in the context of discussing children's learning. This is that the 'small ideas' are children's ideas and may or may not be consistent with the scientific view. Concepts, on the other hand, are expected to be generally accepted ones, known to fit a range of available evidence, whilst children's ideas may not do so. We have to take notice of all children's ideas, whether or not 'correct'.

Which ideas and at what level?

There remain questions about the development of children's ideas.

- Which areas of understanding should we aim to develop?
- How far along the development should we go in the primary school?

As there exists in all the nations of the UK, and in most other countries, a national curriculum which sets out what is to be taught, it would seem that these questions have already been answered. However, it is often difficult to see the lines of development in these official documents, either because they set out *content* rather than *ideas* to be learned, or because by being too detailed they obscure the overall picture.

Table 10.1 presents in a simplified way what is contained in most curriculum requirements. By identifying ideas for early and later development it suggests an overall progression in ideas; and by expressing ideas in terms of relationships it suggests how far to go.

The meaning of early and later development is left flexible; this will depend on when and how much science is taught in the early years. 'Early' is likely to mean the first two or three years of primary science education, whilst 'later' means the end of the primary school, at the age of about 11 or 12.

What has to be emphasised is that to develop a firm grasp of the ideas listed in the table a great deal of exploration across a wide range of experience is required. For example, both the fabric activities of Chapter 2 and the school building activities of Chapter 5 provide experience relating to the concepts under the heading 'Materials, their properties and interactions'. It isn't essential for these particular activities to be used – many others would help the development of the same concepts. This means that neither this list nor most national curriculum statements really restrict choice of content.

Content means the subject matter of an activity or topic; the particular object, materials and events that it concerns (building a model house with wood and cardboard; seeing which fabric is most waterproof; observing the feeding, growth, movement and reproduction of snails, etc.). It should be chosen so that:

Area of understanding	Early development	Later development
The characteristics of living things	• There are different kinds of living things called plants • There are different kinds of living things called animals	• Living things can be grouped according to their general characteristics • Different kinds of plants and animals can be found in different locations • Competition for life-supporting resources determines which survive where • Human activity can interfere in the balance between resources and the plants and animals depending on them
Processes of life	• Plants and animals grow, develop and reproduce themselves and need food, air and water to live • Animals have senses which respond to different signals from the environment • Human beings must have enough of certain kinds of food of healthy growth and activity	• All living things, including human beings, have ways of carrying out the same life processes • Plants need certain conditions to grow and make food • The organs within the body have specific functions • The human body needs certain conditions to remain healthy • Animals and plants depend on each other in various ways
Materials, their properties and interactions	• Materials can be divided into groups such as metals, wood, plastic, with certain properties • Materials vary in properties • Materials are used for different purposes because of their properties	• Materials are classified according to their origins and composition • The properties of materials (including solid, liquid and gas) can be explained by their composition and structure • Manufactured materials can be designed to have required properties • Materials are changed (sometimes reversibly, sometimes irreversibly) through reaction with each other, erosion and energy transfer • The strength of a structure depends on its form as well as the material it is made from
Energy sources, transmission and transfer	• Objects are seen if they give out light or reflect it • Objects that stop light cause shadows • Sounds are caused by objects vibrating • Heating and cooling things can change them	• Seeing things involves light coming from the objects into our eyes • Light passes from one place to another in straight lines but can be made to change direction if things are put in the way • Some materials allow an electric current to pass through them (conductors) • There is always a continuous path of a conducting material when electricity flows from one terminal of a battery to another • Light, sound, electricity, mechanical energy, etc. are forms of energy which can be changed from one form to another • Some sources of energy are renewable but fuels are being used up and so need to be used carefully

Area of understanding	Early development	Later development
Forces and movement	• To make anything move or stop moving, there has to be something pushing, pulling or twisting it • How far something moves in a certain time gives its speed	• Forces are needed to change the shape or the motion of objects • When several forces are acting their effect is combined and if the object is at rest, they cancel each other out • Gravity is the force which pulls objects towards the Earth and this force (the weight) differs in places where gravity is different • It takes more force to start or stop a heavy object moving than a lighter one
The Earth and its place in the Universe	• The sun, moon and Earth are three-dimensional bodies which move relative to each other in regular patterns • There are patterns in the weather • Soil is a mixture of material derived from rocks and living things	• The Earth is surrounded by a layer of air and water vapour which in various conditions produces different kinds of weather • The Earth is one of nine known planets orbiting the Sun • Days, months and years are related to the movements of the Earth, and of the Moon around it • Objects used in everyday life are derived from materials taken from the Earth and their supply is limited

Table 10.1 Ideas developed through primary science (adapted from *Teaching and Learning Primary Science*, Harlen, 1993, p. 145)

• it will motivate and interest the children;

• it gives plenty of opportunity for problem-solving activities and the use of a wide range of skills;

• there are adequate and sufficient resources available;

• it enables children to develop the ideas that the teacher has in mind.

But any one set of activities is not enough on its own; others are required to consolidate the concepts under the one heading. Adding together the activities which might contribute to all the areas of understanding sufficiently to give children the chance to develop ideas through their own activity, the result is more than enough to fill the curriculum time for science throughout the primary school.

What science do teachers need to know?

Setting out in one list or document the ideas to be developed is daunting for many primary teachers who feel that their own understanding of the science is not adequate. However, it should help if we recall that the role of the teacher is not to transmit information to children but to foster the children's skills, ideas and attitude development by:

• planning activities that will motivate children to use process skills in developing their ideas;

• finding out their starting points and adapting activities to link in with their previous experience;

• asking questions that make the children think;

- providing opportunities for discussion and for children to communicate their ideas;

- encouraging critical review of how activities have been carried out and of ways in which this could be improved;

- teaching the skills required to use equipment effectively and the conventions involved in using graphs, tables, symbols in communication.

It cannot be denied that a teacher needs to understand the skills and the 'big' ideas that the activities are planned to develop. Without this he or she can't recognise ideas that are likely to lead in useful directions or ones that will take the children down blind alleys, or ask effective questions or hold discussions that probe and promote understanding. However, this is very different from saying that teachers need understanding so that the scientific ideas can be taught didactically. That could only lead to rote learning and would be severely damaging to children's confidence in their own ability to make sense of their experiences. One thing we know is that the only way children develop ideas that they fully understand is through their own thinking. Teachers can't do the thinking for them, neither can they short-circuit the learning process by presenting the big ideas for children to learn.

If we look in detail at the items in the list above we find several that are related to general teaching skills. As well as knowledge of the subject matter, teaching in any area of the curriculum requires:

- knowledge of how children learn;

- knowledge of how to make a subject interesting and accessible;

- knowledge of classroom management and ways of organising for learning.

This puts the knowledge of the science in perspective, since there is so much besides that is important and that is part of primary teachers' general competence. It doesn't deny the necessity of understanding the science but helps the realisation that teachers already have a great deal of the knowledge that is required besides that of subject matter.

It also helps to point out that the knowledge that is needed is that of the broad principles – the big ideas – not the answers to every question that children might ask. Teachers worry about 'not knowing enough' when they think that teaching means that they must be able to answer children's questions and present accurate information. In practice no-one could answer all the questions that the enquiring minds of children will raise and indeed in many cases it would be wrong to attempt to answer them. Giving children facts which don't link into their own experience and thinking can deter them from asking questions, since they find they can't understand the answers. So teachers have to respond in other ways to questions, turning them wherever possible into ones which the children themselves can investigate, as suggested at the end of Chapter 3.

Experience, supported by research, shows that teachers, as educated adults with a great deal of relevant experience, can quickly grasp broad principles of science at this level. Many teachers have, indeed, developed their own understanding by 'reading up' on topics or by talking to colleagues. Unfortunately the books that are available are often written for other readership and are unsuitable for the purpose of developing primary teachers' understanding. The recognition of this problem is fortunately leading to the creation of more suitable help (as in the background information sections of the Nuffield Primary Science *Teacher's Guides*, 1996) and the provision of in-service courses designed to address the problem. There are now available materials for teachers that give information about children's ideas in a range of topics, which will help teachers plan in advance for what they are likely to find (e.g. PSTS, 1995) and which give help in working from these small ideas towards the bigger ones.

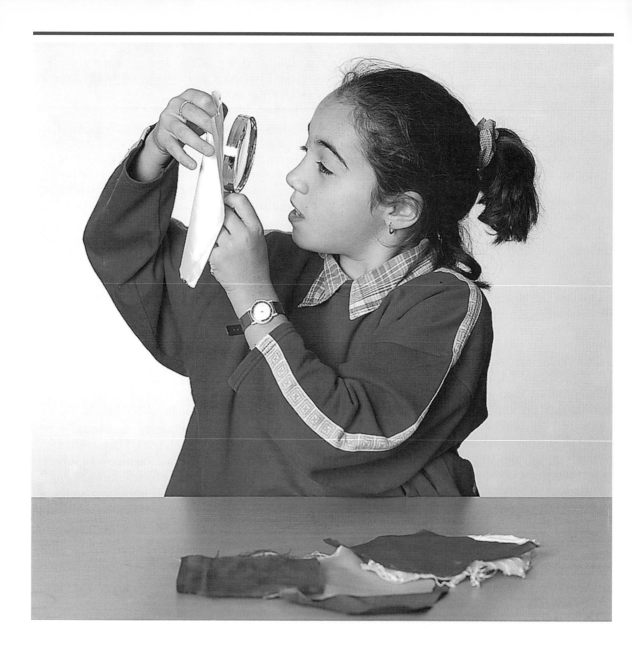

References

Department of Education and Science (DES) (1978) *Primary Education in England*. London: HMSO

Elstgeest, J. (1985) 'Encounter, interaction and dialogue', in W. Harlen (Ed) *Primary Science: Taking the Plunge*. London: Heinemann Educational

Harlen, W. (1993) *Teaching and Learning Primary Science*. London: Paul Chapman

Harlen, W. (1996) *The Teaching of Science in Primary Schools*. London: David Fulton

Harlen, W., Holroyd, C. and Byrne, M. (1995) *Confidence and Understanding in Teaching Science and Technology in Primary Schools*. Edinburgh: Scottish Council for Research in Education

Howe, C.J. (1990) 'Grouping children for effective learning in science', *Primary Science Review*, 13, 26–7

Jelly, S. (1985) 'Helping children raise questions – and answering them', in W. Harlen (Ed) *Primary Science: Taking the Plunge*. London: Heinemann Educational

Masters, G. and Forster, M. (1996) *Developmental Assessment*. Melbourne: Australian Council for Educational Research

Nuffield Primary Science (1996) 11 *Teacher's Guides for Key Stage 1, Teacher's Guides for Key Stage 2*. London: Collins Educational

Primary School Teachers and Science (PSTS) Project (1995) *Understanding Science Concepts*. Oxford: University of Oxford Department of Educational Studies and Westminster College

Science 5/13 Units for Teachers (1972–75) (26 titles). London: Macdonald Educational

Schilling, M., Hargreaves, L., Harlen, W. with Russell, T. (1990) *Assessing Science in the Primary Classroom: Written Tasks*. London: Paul Chapman

Wragg, E. C., Bennett, S.N. and Carre, C. (1989) 'Primary teachers and the National Curriculum', *Research Papers in Education*, Vol. 44, No. 3, 17–37

INDEX